Oppos.

Readings from a Hyphenated Space

Oppositional Aesthetics

Readings from a Hyphenated Space

Arun Mukherjee

TSAR
Toronto
Cardiff
1994

TSAR Publications
P. O. Box 6996, Station A
Toronto, Ontario
M5W 1X7 Canada

The publishers acknowledge generous assistance
from the Ontario Arts Council and the Canada Council.

Canadian Cataloguing in Publication Data

Mukherjee, Arun Prabha, 1946-
   Oppositional aesthetics : readings from a hyphenated space

Includes bibliographical references.
ISBN 0-920661-42-4

1. Canadian literature (English) - Minority authors -
History and criticism - Congresses.* 2. Literature -
Aesthetics. I. Title.

PS8089.5.M46M8 1994   C810.9′8   C94-932588-0
PR9188.2.M55M8 1994

Printed and bound in Canada

Contents

Introduction *vii*

PART ONE: THE COLOUR OF THEORY—
A NON-WHITE READER READS

1. Introduction to *Towards an Aesthetic
of Opposition 3*

2. The "Race Consciousness" of a
South Asian (Canadian, of course) Academic *9*

3. The Vocabulary of the "Universal":
The Cultural Imperialism of the Universalist
Criteria of Western Literary Criticism *17*

4. Ideology in the Classroom:
A Case Study in the Teaching of English
Literature in Canadian Universities *30*

5. The Third World in the Dominant Western
Cinema: Responses of a Third World Viewer *39*

6. Bears and Men in Birney's
"The Bear on the Delhi Road" *49*

7. On Reading Renu:
Text/Language/Culture/Translation *56*

PART TWO: MINORITY CANADIAN WRITING

8. Ironies of Colour in the Great White North:
The Discursive Strategies of Some Hyphenated Canadians *69*

9. South Asian Poetry in Canada: In Search of a Place *80*

10. The Sri Lankan Poets in Canada: An Alternative View *96*

11. The Poetry of Michael Ondaatje
and Cyril Dabydeen: Two Responses to Otherness *112*

12. The Poetry of Rienzi Crusz: Songs of an Immigrant *133*

13. Narrating India:
Rohinton Mistry's *Such a Long Journey 144*

14. *Digging Up the Mountains*:
Bissoondath's Doomed World *152*

15. *A Planet of Eccentrics*: Begamudre's Fantastic India *158*

16. M G Vassanji's *Uhuru Street 164*

17. Writing from a Hard Place:
The African Fiction of M G Vassanji *169*

Notes *179*

Acknowledgements *189*

Introduction

Oppositional Aesthetics: Readings from a Hyphenated Space is an amalgamation of the old and the new. The book pulls together my writings on South Asian Canadian literature as well as pieces that, I believe, are of specific relevance to Canadian culture. All the essays from my earlier book, *Towards an Aesthetic of Opposition*,[1] including the Introduction, are included since people are still asking for that book in the bookstores although it is no longer in print. Over the last two years, I have been asked by a large number of people, Canadians and visiting scholars, as to where they can find it. Many of them have apologized for having photocopied the book in its entirety, given the fact that it was not available for purchase.

I had never imagined that the book would turn out to be such a success. For even before seeing the light of print, the readers for a government funding agency rejected it as being "too angry," a response that was not unique to these privileged readers. (I wonder when one crosses that line of decorum beyond which one is deemed "too" angry.) After the book came out, the dominant media did not review it. And yet, the book found its readers. Their approval and encouragement have been invaluable to me.

Towards an Aesthetic of Opposition and its writer came to be known and discussed as proponents of "oppositional aesthetics." I believe I could not have found a more suitable title for the present volume. My work continues to be oppositional to the dominant ideologies of literary and cultural analysis in Euro-America. This oppositionality is directed against dominant ways of perceiving literature that were drilled into me as a student and that continue to wield enormous influence to this day even though they have been challenged by a diverse set of constituencies such as writers and critics in the Third World, and feminists, racial-minority, gay and poststructuralist critics and theorists in the West. I have felt empowered by their challenges to the dominant ways of doing literary criticism, and yet I have also had some disagreements with the dissonant voices in the West when they have indulged in subtler forms of universalizing while theoretically decrying it (for instance, the tendency of these avant-garde critics to treat Freudian and Lacanian theories of human behaviour as though they were universal).

Many people who love reading have told me that they were turned off the academic study of literature because it seemed to have no room for incorporating why they liked reading literary works in the first place. My own responses to works of literature were often disallowed by the overall climate of the profession. For instance, while I responded to a work of fiction on the basis of what I would call my ethical consciousness, the academic papers that I had to produce were based on the so-called formal aspects of the work. I wondered why the critical work on a book ignored aspects that seemed the most important to me, such as poverty, exploitation, social inequality, social and political conflict, imperialism and racism (gender as a separate category came much later for me).

Basically, it was the moral passion, or what one might call social consciousness, of the writer that engaged me most deeply in literary texts. I cannot admire a literary work as though it were a "well wrought urn," to use Cleanth Brooks's famous phrase. Literature is too often discussed in terms of metaphors of food or as objets d'art. Literature, for me, is not a "confection" to be admired for its taste and texture. Rather, in Kenneth Burke's phrase, literature is "equipment for living." It is someone speaking rather than a cold, dead objet d'art. And, because it is someone speaking, it is about human beings living in the world and reporting on how they live. I read literature for the tone of this voice speaking. Is it complacent, self-enclosed, unaware of its privilege? Or does it convey a spectrum of emotions: empathy, pity, guilt, shame, anger, love, mockery, joy, sorrow?

And yet the critical analyses that I was taught to produce and the models that I was asked to learn from seldom engaged with such aspects of the text. Indeed, to pay attention to such things was pejoratively called "sociological" and we were amply warned not to produce any analyses that smacked of such tendencies. As students of literature, our job was to pay attention to the texture of language, to tropes and figures of speech, to symbols and imagery, and to form and structure. Yes, it was permitted to speak of the characters in the text, but only in terms of their passage from innocence to experience or in terms of their personal relationships. Anything else was deemed "political" and hence outside the purview of "literature." Although I know that these attitudes are not dead yet, I have used the past tense to speak of them because they no longer enjoy total dominance.

I and many of my class fellows went through graduate school with a split consciousness. I felt a strange disjunction between my gut responses to a text and the "proper" language I had to use to produce an analysis acceptable to my professors so that I could get a good grade and remain in graduate school. I and some of my contemporaries went through graduate school always a little uneasy about whether we had spotted the key symbols and images in a text and whether we had figured out the structure underlying it. To my utter mortification, I could never figure out the preferred response on my own. I made up for my shortcomings by finding out what the eminent critic or reviewer had said about the text in question and regurgitating it.

It is hard to pinpoint that transformative moment when I found my own voice and was no longer afraid of authority. It happened for me with the help of two Marxist critics: Raymond Williams and Kenneth Burke. Yes, they were male and white and not at all astute on race and gender. But during the twenty-year siege that was my education in literary analysis, they were the only two voices of dissent, unsanctioned by my university, that gave me permission to think about literature as a comment on human life in all its ramifications.

Thus, my professional radicalization did not come about through feminist literary theory. While it was exhilarating for me to read Kate Millett's *Sexual Politics*, mainly because of her disrespect for the rules of academic decorum, I also felt quite uncomfortable with her text's lapses into xenophobia.[2] I feel that way about a lot of feminist literary theory. Its project of "recovering" and interpreting women's writing has often rubbed me and many other women of colour the wrong way. Shaped as my consciousness is by the fact of having been born a non-white British subject, anticolonial, anti-imperialist, and antiracist struggles are of the utmost importance to me and any feminism which ignores these realities is of no use to me.

I have been teaching Women's Studies courses now for at least ten years. I taught many canonical women's texts during this period that upset me on account of their attitudes to things such as colonialism, racism, and classism. While texts such as Aphra Behn's *Oroonoko*, Charlotte Perkins Gilman's *Herland*, Kate Chopin's *The Awakening*, and Margaret Atwood's *Handmaid's Tale* alienate me as a non-white woman reader because they diminish non-white people's humanity, and while I can testify to similar responses from many of my students and acquaintances, I feel dispirited that new work continues to be produced on these and other women writers that does not pay any attention to the "isms" that I mentioned earlier.

Even though feminism and feminist literary theory are seen as radical discourses, I, as a non-white woman am forced to retain an oppositional stance to them as well. I often find that texts that I consider utterly demeaning to me and other Third World people's humanity are being taught and written about as feminist classics. I would like to narrate an anecdote here to convey a sense of my day-to-day struggles.

When I came to York University in 1985, two of the courses I was asked to teach had Charlotte Perkins Gilman's *Herland* on the reading list. The senior colleague who was explaining the courses to me asked me what I thought of this particular text. When I said that I had never heard of it, he told me enthusiastically that it was a recently "recovered" feminist classic and that its radical analysis of women's condition would blow my mind away, given the fact that it was written in 1915.

Well, I began reading the text with great enthusiasm. But halfway into the text, I recoiled in horror as the text wiped out all the non-white women in order to create the racially pure utopia of Herland. Hadn't, I wondered, my senior colleague noticed this textual genocide? When I went to the library to do more research on Gilman and her texts, in the inordinate amount of research that feminist critics have produced on Gilman, I did not find a single piece of work that acknowledged, let alone criticize, Gilman for her fanatical brand of racism.

It took me almost two years to articulate my response to Gilman's racism and to the feminist theory that is blind to this racism.[3] However, the following response of a reviewer to my critique of racist tendencies of certain feminist foremothers in "A House Divided" suggests to me that divisions in feminist circles run deep and communication does not always succeed in removing our disagreements:

> Mukherjee would have us disavow the early white feminists, whom we have only just discovered, because they colluded with "racist and imperialist forces of the time." This seems like a very tall order. If we investigate the values of most historical figures who lived prior to last week, of colour or white, we will find racial biases, homophobia, and ethnocentrism. Shall we discard them all and spin, rootlessly, in the winds of history? Or take their values into account, then ferret out what we can learn from them as sisters under the skin? We will lose the battle if we don't find ways of living together in the trenches.[4]

Now I had never demanded that we do not read these women who, I said, "colluded with the racist and imperialist forces of the time." In fact, I believe that we need to read such texts, albeit in small doses, in order to keep our historic memory alive. I had simply demanded that they not be written about and taught in a tone of breathless celebration that they have been accorded. This reviewer's words, as well as plenty of work that continues to be published on writers like Gilman, Chopin, Charlotte Bronte and our own Sarah Jeanette Duncan once again underline for me how wide the gulf of misunderstanding is between those who find racism and colonialism in women's writing objectionable and those who do not notice it.

I have spent so much time talking about my discomfort with feminist theory here because it positions itself as an oppositional discourse in relation to "male studies." For those of us who are not white, things do not change a lot if we substitute dead white male authors with dead white female authors. Nor is substitution or inclusion enough. The "add and stir" method of curriculum building does not have room for conflict and contradictions. It assumes that white European authors and non-white non-European authors can be mixed and matched and taught according to the theoretical norms based upon the analyses of white canonical writers. Although inclusion is better than total silence, the outcome of applying eurocentric criteria to texts of nonwhite writers is total distortion of these texts. What kind of violence is done to non-European writing when critics and teachers lack cross-cultural understanding is perhaps best captured by Chinua Achebe's recounting of the following experience:

> I received two very touching letters from high-school children in Yonkers, New York, who—bless their teacher—had just read *Things Fall Apart*. One of them was particularly happy to learn about the customs and superstitions of an African tribe. . . .
>
> The young fellow from Yonkers, perhaps partly on account of his age but I believe also for much deeper and more serious reasons, is obviously unaware that the life of his own tribesmen in Yonkers, New York, is full of odd customs and superstitions and, like everybody else in his culture, imagines that he needs a trip to Africa to encounter those things.[5]

Achebe's comments alert us to the fact many postcolonial critics overlook: that simply teaching Third World literary texts does not change consciousness. That perhaps consciousness needs to be changed *before* the non-Western literary text can be appreciated. And yet, "postcolonial literature" and "postcolonial theory" are discussed ad nauseam without paying attention to the problem of the cultural borders and communication gaps they create. As a reader and teacher of literatures from the Third World, I am therefore forced to take an oppositional stance to the naming and teaching of these literatures under the rubric of "postcolonial literature." I focus on the problems I face as an academic assigned by the institution to teach "postcolonial literature" in my forthcoming book, "A Sign Called Postcolonial: The Teaching and Theorizing of Third World Literatures in the Western Academy."

Thus, a large part of my critical work has emerged from my struggles with the dominant cultural discourses that impinge upon my existence as a nonwhite woman who was born in preindependence India. While I struggle along with the white feminist critics in challenging the hegemony of dead white male voices, I also have to struggle against them when their examples of "women's experience" are all drawn from a small group of white middle-class women. Similarly, although the "postcolonial" critics and I are together on many theoretical and practical concerns, I must protest against their homogenizing of literatures from non-Western cultures.

If it was simply an intellectual struggle where I spoke out my disagreements with other scholars in a dialogical mode, it would have been fun. However, it has not been fun because the literary institution does not provide equal access to all points of view. If one does not write in sanctioned ways, one does not get published in the right places. And if one does not get published in the right places, i.e., refereed journals or university presses, one does not get a tenure-stream job. I have had to wait until forty-four years of age to get that coveted job since I did not meet the above-mentioned criteria.

Writing, therefore, is not just a matter of putting one's thoughts on paper. Writing is also about social power. How I write depends a lot on who I write for. One of the saving graces of my life has been the advent of *TheToronto South Asian Review* (now reincarnated as *The Toronto Review*). I have been able to write in it without anxiety and in my own voice. Similarly, the emergence of presses like the now defunct Williams-Wallace, Sister Vision and TSAR made room for those of us who felt stifled by the prevalent modes of literary and cultural analyses.

These small presses and their authors have brought down the fortifications erected by the Canadian literary establishment and changed the face of the Canadian literary landscape. Both the entity called "Canadian literature," and the essentialized Canadian identity it was premised on has been seriously eroded. The hyphenated Canadians, as those of us who are not from the "two founding nations" have been called, have challenged their otherization by the unitary notions of national identity and asserted that being "different" by no means equates with being un-Canadian. Racial and ethnic minority writers, particularly aboriginal writers, have been at the forefront in the task of rethinking and reformulating the meaning of Canada as a nation state. One aspect of these reformulations has been to force those in the business of Canlit to rethink the

Canadian canon.

Built in accordance with the goals of Canadian nationalism, the (English) Canlit canon has had certain invisible rules that exclude non-Anglo writers. Far too often, works dealing with minority racial and ethnic groups have been described as "immigrant," "ethnic," or "new," all labels that stigmatize those thus identified as "un-Canadian." On the other hand, first-generation Anglo writers have found acceptance easily. (Michael Ondaatje, Joseph Skvorecky, and Neil Bissoondath are exceptions to this pattern, and the reason for their acceptance by the mainstream, I believe, is ideological compatibility.) As M G Vassanji once told me, while no one considers Margaret Atwood's *Handmaid's Tale* and Janette Turner Hospital's *The Ivory Swing* un-Canadian because they are set in the United States and India respectively, his and other racial minority writers' works have been dismissed as un-Canadian because they are set outside Canada.

An aspect of such biases is the absence of racial and ethnic minority writers on Canlit reading lists. Another is the lack of critical attention to their work. So, while there is so much critical work on a few select Canadian authors that book-length bibliographies are available on them, others don't even get a review. Still others, like Farida Karodia and S S Dhami, have not even had the luck to find Canadian publishers and have had to go abroad to publish their work.

This is a very sad state of affairs. For I believe that writers of one's own ethnic group have some thing special to say to one. I do not make this argument on essentialist notions of "blood kinship" but on the basis of shared social experience and historical memory. As a Canadian who originated in India, I read the works of South Asian Canadian writers to learn about our community's experience in Canada and its different migrations from India to Africa, the Caribbean and North America. That is a knowledge that no other body of literature can provide for me.

Of course, the "must read" nature of my interest in South Asian Canadian literature does not mean that I am not interested in other Canadian and other national literatures. All I am arguing for is the acknowledgement of the ethnicity-based relationship between readers and writers and to draw on this relationship in redesigning and delivering the curriculum of Canlit. While I believe that all learning must start with learning about one's own background, it must not stop there but go on to include one's fellow beings in enlarging concentric circles, beginning with communities that comprise the Canadian nation state and on to the rest of the world. Since life is short and one cannot learn everything that one would like to, we need a lot of discussion to decide the curriculum for our young people to ensure that they get a chance to learn about themselves as well as about the richness and diversity of cultures across the globe.

This is not possible yet. For instance, an Italian-Canadian student of mine told me that several of them had been trying to get a course set up in Italian-Canadian literature but got nowhere. I hope some day we will be able to think about curriculum in such a way that we can encourage and reward students for reading and researching writers of their own ethnic background. I would like those Italian-Canadian students to be able to do a credit course in Italian-Canadian writing, just as I would like students from other ethnic groups to have a similar possibility. Of course new and creative ways of thinking about the curriculum and its delivery have to be devised before such courses can become a reality.

Oppositional Aesthetics is a small step towards that future. I began reading South Asian Canadian literature as the result of a happy accident. In 1981, as I sat unemployed with a PhD in American literature, Dr Suwanda Sugunasiri offered me a part-time job to work on a Secretary of State-funded project on the literature of South Asian Canadians. Encountering these works was meaningful to me in two profound ways: first, as a South Asian Canadian person and, secondly, as a literary critic who had to think from ground zero to write about them. The essays included in this book are the result of my struggle with the questions of ethnicity, reader response and literary value, among other things.

When I first encountered the writings of South Asian Canadians, I did so without the benefit of the current debates on race, ethnicity, gender, sexual orientation and their impact on reading and ascribing of value. While I have learned, and continue to learn, a lot from these debates, I feel that they seldom descend from the plane of abstraction. If we do not pay attention to actual works that wrestle with these issues and the concrete situations that they illuminate, theoretical sophistication begins to look like clever game-playing.

Oppositional Aesthetics is not antitheoretical but my theorizations are tentative and provisional. I begin with my personal response to literature and literary criticism in the context of my situation in the world as a South Asian Canadian woman and hope that there is enough in my situation that can be shared or empathized with by others. I hope that the book will find such readers and that they will find it useful.

A few words about the context of the new essays included here. Many of them were written as reviews for publication in the *Toronto South Asian Review*. Others were written at the invitations of conference organizers to participate in conversations going on in the academic world. Unlike the academics of previous generations, I have not had the luxury of taking up a major project and working on it in the isolation of my study. I would like the reader to remember that these pieces are not sui generis but improvizations on themes supplied by others. That, I guess, is the nature of academic writing.

However, I do hope that this "academic writing" is not "academic" in the derogatory sense of that word, i.e., "scholarly to the point of being unaware of the outside world" (Heritage Dictionary). I would like to hope that I speak in an accessible language and about issues that are not merely "theoretical." Whether I have succeeded in my aim is for the reader to judge.

PART ONE

THE COLOUR OF THEORY—

A NON-WHITE READER READS

1. Introduction to

'Towards an Aesthetic of Opposition'[1]

These essays are written by a person who was born and brought up in postcolonial India, had a thoroughly colonial education, both in India and at the University of Toronto, and then went through a painful and difficult process of decolonization. The essays record the dialectics of that struggle. In a sense, it is a collective struggle, being waged in the hearts and minds of all Third World people.

My education, like that of most of my generation, had been from top down. Knowledge trickled down to us from the West and we paid respectful homage to every printed word that bore a Western name. When we did not understand something—and there was a lot that did not make sense—we blamed ourselves for our lack of knowledge.

Thus, a canon made mostly of ahistorical and apolitical Anglo-American texts was presented to me as the epitome of what consti-tuted literature. It did not educate me in anything and alienated me from my reality. It made me believe that literature pertained to the cultivation of certain emotions—sentimental effusions over the beauty of nature, anguish over mutability—and a high-minded dis-dain for all rationality and abstract thought.

My Canadian education did not remove any cobwebs. Professors and fellow-students seemed to talk ad infinitum about symbolism and imagery, trace elaborate structures and patterns that persist-ently remained invisible to me. Every hero and heroine seemed to go on a quest of discovery of self-identity in their discourses. The other thing these heroes did was to go through initiations of some sort. At times these were called rites of passage. And yes, there were some other themes: modern sensibility, i.e., the pain of living in a Godless universe, wilderness versus civilization and their endless pulls, creativity versus madness, and, finally, the celebration of complexity that perpetually wrings its hands in the face of the grandeur and terror of the universe. Their reiteration soon made me realize that the reason why the trickle of knowledge that I had drunk from in India had not made sense to me was not because there was more of it that I did not know but because the trickle remained substantively the same even when I stood close to the fount.

To discover intricate patterns for their own sake has never interested me. However, one churned out the kinds of papers that one was asked for if one wanted to get through a highly punitive and exclusive system.

In order for these petty, irresponsible and elitist schemes to work, the curriculum is so chosen as to exclude or ghettoize dissonant discourses. In India, the United States Information Service provided us, free of charge, American literature anthologies edited by Robert E Spiller et al. F O Matthiessen's *The American Renaissance* was the other text that the USIS supplied in multiple copies to our departmental library.

As a result, I imbibed an attitude that American writers were all latter day Romantics, communing with nature and leading a conflict-free life in a beautiful land. Without any historical background, I read *The Adventures of Huckleberry Finn* and took it to be another idyll. The historical traumas of slavery and the fate of the native peoples were kept obscure from my mind.

The University of Toronto did not shake me out of my misconceptions. Here, too, one studied about poets and novelists who wrote about the travails of the spirit, their yearning for a lost paradise, their disgust with modern times, and so on. We were constantly told to remember that "it isn't what you say but how you say it that's important." What you say is not important, apparently, because themes are supposedly perennial—love, hate, coming of age, cycles of nature, death.

Obviously, the themes of history—conquest and subjugation, anticolonial struggles, racism, sexism, class conflict—are all absent from this worldview. Hence, the works that deal with this worldview are also largely absent from the curricula of departments of English in Canada. The shrines at which they worship are to be seen in their course offerings. T S Eliot, Henry James, James Joyce, Ezra

4

Pound, Robert Frost, and Wallace Stevens dominate modern literature curricula.

Hegemony is thus achieved, on the one hand by a careful selection of artists, and on the other by neglecting the socio-political contexts and concentrating exclusively on technique. Elsewhere, I have examined in greater detail the distortions this kind of attention to technique, completely isolated from context, creates.[2] The text is read passively, on its own terms and never for identifying the exclusions or affiliations it exercises.

When these halls of learning do open up to such fields as Commonwealth literature, Black literature, Women's Studies, they do two things to them. On the one hand, these courses are marginalized in various ways so that the students know in no uncertain terms their relative unimportance in the scheme of things, and, on the other, their effectiveness is undermined because they are often taught and written about using the same ahistorical methods I have mentioned earlier. A majority of the white critics writing and teaching about Third World writers flatten them down to their image patterns, mythic archetypes, allusions, intertextuality, East-West conflicts and, ultimately, universality.

I want to say here, as so many other voices of the Third World are saying, that this condescending and ignorant approach is tiresome. We are tired of being told what is great literature and how it ought to be read. We are amazed how these institutions of learning in the West go on ignoring our responses to Western literature and literary criticism. We are astonished at the way they choose to read and distort the cultural productions of the Third World artists.

In *Harder They Come*, Michael Thelwell describes how the young audiences in the slums of Jamaica appropriate the Hollywood Western to suit their own needs. "The movies were still a great part of their scene, but now they shouted for the Indians and never took the white man's side, much less his name."[3] A similar rereading and appropriation or rejection of Western canonical texts is a very important aspect of the oppositional critical activity going on in the Third World.

Another aspect of Third World literary and critical activity is the creation of new artistic modes that break away from the Western artist-as-hero-creating-in-the-isolation-of-his-soul type of works.

The Third World artists create to give voice to the experience of their community, to bring to life the historic memory and to explore the future. They deliberately reject the ahistorical Western modes. Thus, in *Meridian*, a novel of struggle and pride of identity, Alice Walker's comment subtly brings out the difference between the two modes of creativity: "Anne-Marion, she knew, had become a well-known poet whose poems were about her two children, and the quality of the light that fell across a lake she owned."[4]

These oppositional critiques are winning audiences, whether the gatekeepers of the universities admit them or not. There are only two ways to go. One is to listen and debate; perhaps both sides will change and learn in that process. The other, the one that prevails now, is to pretend that no other voices speak and to continue to teach, read, and write in one's hermetically sealed box. Let the black parents scream about racism in *The Adventures of Huckleberry Finn*. We will continue to teach it as a classic. And we will continue to exclude texts that the blacks themselves have written. And, yes, we will talk about the spectre of censorship when we hear such talk.

The essays collected in this volume have all emerged in a combative spirit. The stance of establishment literary criticism in North America is appreciative. The literary critics choose the works that have engaged them and then carry on detailed analyses, never doubting for a moment that what pleases them may not please everybody else. Thus, an upper-middle-class, usually male and white, point of view is presented with the authority of the universal. I, of course, do not have that authority. I cannot afford to speak in a calm and collected voice. The stance of these essays is confrontational, not out of choice but out of necessity. I have tried to point out how the dominant discourse in North America dehistoricizes and depoliticizes everything so that non-white, non-male, working-class ways of apprehending reality seldom get a hearing.

Though the essays speak for themselves, it would be helpful if the reader knew the contexts they emerged from. While the arrangement in the book is tactical, here I would like to pursue the chronological link.

"The Poetry of Michael Ondaatje and Cyril Dabydeen: Two Responses to Otherness" came out of a project on South Asian writing in Canada. The paper emerged only because I was forced to place Ondaatje in the context of other South Asian writers active in Canada. I began to ask questions like why had no other South Asian writer received the critical attention as that bestowed on Ondaatje by Canadian white critics? Why had they not bothered to check reviews by fellow Sri Lankans? Why had no other South Asian writers got well-known publishers and fancy get-up? The paper is an attempt to seek out for myself the factors that would attract white critics to Ondaatje's work.

"South Asian Poetry in Canada: In Search of a Place" and "The Poetry of Rienzi Crusz: Songs of an Immigrant" were completed after "Two Responses to Otherness," although the research and mental processes evident in the three essays belong to the same spectrum. The three papers, I believe, are complementary, and some of the unstated meanings and assumptions will become clear to the reader simply through juxtaposing the three.

"The Sri Lankan Poets in Canada: An Alternative View" emerged from similar concerns and was written at the invitation of the guest editor of *The Toronto South Asian Review*'s special issue on Sri Lanka. Once again, placing Ondaatje in a group setting brought out questions that would remain muted if one focussed on the single author. Here I also wanted to examine the damaging impact of Western critical assumptions on the creativity of Third World writers.

"The Vocabulary of the 'Universal': The Cultural Imperialism of the Universalist Criteria of Western Literary Criticism" was written in the white heat of anger that I felt upon reading the quotation from Northrop Frye that was chosen as the theme for the 1984 conference of the Canadian Association for Commonwealth Literature and Language Studies (CACLALS). I felt that the whole conference was being based on the assumption that Third World literary works could be read as derivative and inter-textually linked with the works of the Western European tradition.

"Ideology in the Classroom: A Case Study in the Teaching of English Literature in Canadian Universities" was written right after the article on cultural imperialism. I was frustrated by the essays my students at the University of Regina had turned out on a very political story by Margaret Laurence and the paper was an attempt at clarification for myself and, I hoped, for others. For if one cannot communicate one's point of view to others, one hasn't really clarified anything.

"*Digging Up the Mountain* Bissoondath's Doomed World" was done as a book review for *World Literature Written in English*. The conventions of a book review determined the form of the writing and I did not bring in some of the issues bothering me about Neil Bissoondath. Once again, I found it interesting that after Ondaatje, only Bissoondath had managed to find a reputable Canadian publisher. Once again, the Canadian literary community had showered a lot of attention. Bissoondath was also considered good enough to be chosen as a finalist for a prestigious award. I found it curious that the fact of his being V S Naipaul's nephew was loudly announced on the dust jacket of the book as well as taken up in the reviews. I would have liked the discussion to be based on the questions dealing with his art and the politics he projects through his work.

I believe that the context of any writing is important. When I presented these papers at conferences, many unspoken issues came out in the discussions afterwards. I wonder why those issues should emerge only informally and not be written about so that a frank and open discussion can take place across the board. The information I have provided in this Introduction escaped the reach of the written word because of the conventions one must follow if one wants to be listened. Ultimately, one's audience decides how one will write.

I am thankful to journals like *JCL, WLWE* and *TSAR* for providing space for an alternative point of view. I am also thankful to organizations like CACLALS that are open to marginalized people and marginalized issues in ways larger professional organizations of university academics in my discipline are not. The essays collected here would not have seen the light of the day but for these forums. I am especially thankful to Professor Doug Killam and Moyez Vassanji for their constant support for and interest in my work.

Finally, I owe a particular debt of gratitude to Ann Wallace, who considers these essays important enough to be collected and published in book form. Her publishing house, Williams-Wallace, is the right place for the collection to come out from: alongwith works by other people of colour, discovering their history, rediscovering their identity, and struggling for their just place in Canadian society. This book is a part of that collective struggle.

2. The "Race Consciousness" of a South Asian (Canadian, of course) Female Academic

Two years ago, as I was walking on my way to the class, a South Asian male, perhaps in his mid-thirties, asked me for directions to a building. He had chosen me as his informant, I thought, because of our common past: we both could tell by looking at each other that we were South Asians. Anyway, he looked lost and I was only too happy to instruct him. Now such a nondescript encounter would surely have faded from my memory except for this man's next question: "So what courses are you taking?" Why, I asked myself, had this man decided that I could only be a student, despite my very grey head of hair? The answer I gave myself was painful to articulate and is painful to write about: he cannot imagine a South Asian woman in the role of an academic because they are such a rarity on Canadian campuses.

After this internal debate, I told my compatriot: "I teach here." There was surprise and contrition writ large on his face as we parted after he had said his "Oh, I see." And as for me, I pondered over the complexities of my answer for the next few minutes. Although the man's facial expression had changed from registering a desire for familiarity to a combination of awe and admiration, I felt that his admiration would soon disappear if he were to know that I only taught as a part-timer, liable to be hired and fired at the whim of the people who made those decisions.

I still have to pinch myself to remember that my fortunes have changed since then. In fact, as I write this on July 1, 1991, the first day of my first full-time tenure-stream job, the 124th birthday of Canada, I cannot but help connect my personal fortunes with that of the non-white Canadians in general. For I am fully aware that my present success is the outcome of not just my "merit"—that hallowed principle so often invoked by those who claim that employment equity will flood our institutions with "inferior" appointees—but of the antiracist struggles waged across Canada by communities that have borne the brunt of racism in Canada.

My active involvement in this ongoing struggle and my memory of the past struggles are the factors that constitute my race consciousness. Some celebrity academics put the word *race* in quotation marks because there is no such thing in biology as race. We all share the same blood types and the same gene pool. They warn us about essentialisms if we talk about race: things like black people having rhythm in their blood and oriental people being good at math.

My race consciousness, my awareness of the fact that I am non-white in a white country, is certainly not essentialist. I am conscious of being non-white, of being South Asian (I cannot call myself Indian in Canada though that's what I really am), of being "Paki," to the same measure that white Canadians are not conscious of their whiteness. They would rather be "just Canadians."

But being "just Canadian" is a privilege only white people enjoy in Canada. It is we non-whites who are seen as deviants from the norm. So we are tagged with identity cards, some worn proudly, others with resentment. I can't, of course, speak for all non-white Canadians (we even disagree with the words that are used to mark our difference: some find "non-white" totally unpalatable because it is rooted in negation; some love to use the term "people of colour," others hate it because, in their mind, it obliterates our heterogeneity; some have no problem with "visible minority," they say, because one should call a spade a spade, whereas others find it a term imposed by a racist state) but I am always conscious of my being non-white and how that fact determines my total life experience. I doubt that I will ever become "just Canadian," whatever that means.

As to the negative qualifier in "non-white," I have absolutely no problems with that. After all, terms like "nonviolence," "noncooperation," and "civil disobedience" also use negation. Moreover, "non-white" is only one aspect of my multiple identities, for I am also a woman of colour, a Third Worlder, a South Asian, an east Indian, an Indian, a Punjabi, and a Mukherjee (my patronymic caste marker). What term I use to describe myself and my subject matter depends on who I am speaking to and what I am talking about.

(Some white academics have told me that I cannot be a Third Worlder and a South Asian at the same time. One has gone so far as to write that since I have a "comfortable" tenure-stream job, I cannot claim a Third World identity. If I were to use an analogy, this kind of thinking suggests to me that one ceases being a sister or a daughter if one becomes a wife or a mother.) I use the term "non-white" in order to talk about the binary relationship of power where "white" is the dominant term because there is no denying the fact that we live in a racist world order.

Being non-white in an academic setting means, or has meant thus far (I am banking a whole lot on employment equity) being the single non-white, male or female, at departmental meetings or social get-togethers or conferences. It has meant a tremendous loneliness of spirit because your white colleagues don't seem to notice that there is any thing abnormal in a meeting room or a plenary at a conference where only a handful (or less) of non-white people are present (I deliberately use the words "white colleagues" because the non-whites present at such gatherings always talk to each other about the "absence" of people of colour).

My having entered through the gates that have been locked to people who have dark skins, then, becomes an existential and intellectual problem. How have I managed to get in, I ask myself, when so many of my non-white contemporaries with academic ambitions did not make it? And now that I am here, what do I intend to do?

First of all, I intend to survive. In fact, I am here because I knew how to dissemble, to give them what they wanted so that they would give me my degree. That meant never reading a book by a non-white writer as part of the curriculum during my entire education in English literature (both in Canada and India). I try to look back on those days of my studenthood and reconstruct what I thought about the absence of non-white authors in the curriculum. I think again and again of the all-white American Literature courses that I was taught, both in India and Canada, and my unproblematic acceptance of their normalcy.

I realize now the power of the teacher as authority figure. My teachers made the racist, exclusionary curriculum normal for me. They made it normal by convincing me that the curriculum was composed of the "best" works ever written by "man." And whatever did not make it in the canon was not excluded because of racism or sexism but because of objective criteria that measure excellence. Not that I, or my class mates, ever asked any questions about why so-and-so was not on the book list. Messages about exclusion and inclusion, however, were embedded in the discourse of critical theory that we got in the class and in the books we were asked to read.

Racism has a long reach and my soul trembles to think of how much I had imbibed unconsciously. For example, during all my twenty-five years of living in India, I never knew that the United States (Canada was not part of my curriculum at all) also had people of colours other than white. No one, that is my parents, teachers, media, ever told me of the existence of these non-white Americans. The pictures in the papers and magazines were always of white Americans and the books in my curriculum were by them. (Here I can't resist a story Marie Marulé, a Native woman from Alberta told me. When she told people in Zimbabwe (then Rhodesia) that she was a Native Canadian, i.e. "Red Indian," they responded, "But you are extinct"!) Well, that was the silent message my anthologies of American literature gave me too. And it was reinforced by the white visiting professors of American literature and white Peace Corps volunteers.

As a non-white female academic, I intend to make sure that my students will not go away with such unconscious racism unchallenged. Even when I have had no control on the design and content of the courses, I have told my students what I thought of the materials I had been assigned to teach. I began a course I taught on "American Literature" as a part-timer by telling my students who was not on it: Native writers, African American writers, and women writers, both white and non-white. And I made the absence of these writers on the prescribed curriculum a constant presence by invoking them as we read the sanctioned writers. (When I read the course evaluations later, there were two that said that there was too much about racism in the course and not enough about "technique.")

I have had to resort to similar strategies when faced with "Women's Studies" courses that did not include a word about the histories and texts of non-white women. I have told my students to be wary of accepting the experiences of white women as the "universal" experience of *all* women. I have told them that I cannot rejoice with the celebratory histories of Canadian women that present white women getting the vote as "women get the vote," ignoring the fact that Canadians of Native, Chinese, Japanese, and South Asian ancestries, both male and female, had to wait a long time to enjoy voting rights. I have told them about the racism of such prominent feminist foremothers as Charlotte Perkins Gilman and Nellie McClung (whose racism is the reason I can't feel as enthusiastic about Persons' Day as some white feminists). Such questioning of the curriculum leads my students to think about the enveloping cloud of racism in which we live as a society. It makes them suspicious of the curriculum that their society in the shape of their schools, universities and teachers imparts to them.

In fact, some time during the course of teaching, the question always crops up if any of my students have had non-white teachers before taking my course. The number of students who say yes to this question has been infinitesimally small thus far. That question leads us to ask who controls knowledge and how they define it. We talk about the eurocentric nature of the Canadian university and how few and far between are the courses offered on non-European (read non-white) cultures. We talk about whether it is possible to read texts by non-white writers, both male and female, in the framework of aesthetic theories developed in Euro-America.

I am delighted to see that the work we do in my classes also rubs off on the other work my students do. For instance, while reading Attia Hosain's *Sunlight on a Broken Column*, we noticed that the plot treated the servants in the household as characters in their own right. We went on to discuss such classics as Jane Austen's *Pride and Prejudice* where large dinners are eaten in feudal homes with not a servant in sight as though the dinner had cooked and served itself! We also discussed Virginia Woolf's *To the Lighthouse* where servants can appear only off stage and not as part of the plot.

The South Asian text, thus, helps my students envision other ways of writing, other ways of creating and responding to art, and other ways of living. It takes them away from the "universalist" aesthetic norms that actually theorize on the basis of hand-picked "great" works of Euro-America, albeit with my theoretical help. For it is not the text itself which can help them reach across the cultural barriers. (As Chinua Achebe tells us, a letter from a New York high-school student, who had just read his classic text *Things Fall Apart*, thanked him profusely for writing such an informative book on the superstitions and customs of an African tribe, thus defeating the project of the text and its author thoroughly.) So it is my responsibility to challenge my students, both through my teaching and my research, to stop applying "Western" norms and "Western" values as though they were true for all times and all places. When one does that, one does not really encounter the complexity of cultural diversity across our planet but only stares at oneself in the mirror. My goal as a teacher and a researcher has been to challenge this "Western" narcissism, this fake universalism which is really Euro-American ethnocentrism talking about itself in the vocabulary of "the human condition" at the same time that it denies the humanity of others.

I am, thus, always conscious of the "difference" that my being South Asian in a white Canada continuously produces, both inside me and outside of me. I am conscious of the fact that until 1947, the year of India's independence, the doors of Canada were closed to me. I cannot forget that Canada's racist immigration laws pertaining to South Asians were repealed only after the Indian Prime Minister, Jawahar Lal Nehru, personally asked the Canadian government to get rid of them if they wanted a friendly relationship with India. I cannot forget the *Komagata Maru* incident, when Canada quarantined 400 South Asians on this ship for two months, denied them food and water rations and a fair judicial process and finally sent them back, some to their deaths at British hands. I cannot forget this incident even though I did not read it in Canada's history books.

I won't forget these facts, and other such facts pertaining to Native Canadians, Chinese Canadians, Caribbean Canadians and Japanese Canadians until I begin to see real changes happen. I won't forget them until I see Canadian schools teach about *all* Canadians, something they didn't do in my own son's case. I won't forget them until I see Canadian universities open their doors to all Canadians and teach and produce research about all Canadians.

It is funny how some things stick in one's mind while so much else disappears with the flow of time. Twenty years ago, soon after my arrival in Canada as a student, I was asked to visit an elementary school. The children I spoke to were Grade Four and Five students, no older than ten or eleven years. One of the very first things they asked me was why India didn't solve its food problem by eating all the cows that wandered every where in the country. I must say that I was absolutely stunned by the question and the way it was phrased. It assumed that Indians were so foolish that they could not see a solution to their problems that was staring right in their face! It showed a total disregard of the economy and culture of the country that they knew nothing about and it showed an arrogance about their own intellectual superiority. For instance, it would not occur to these children, and their teachers, that the cows may not be "wandering" but "foraging." And that, of course, changes the whole picture. (For those wanting to know more about India's cow-based economy, I recommend Marvin Harris's *Cows, Pigs, Wars and Witches: The Riddles of Cultures.* Harris shows that a living cow in India is far more valuable economically than a dead cow.)

I learnt more about this arrogance when I read Ontario's secondary school textbooks to find out how they represented my part of the world. They told the students about the customs and superstitions of the Indian people and blamed these for India's poverty. I learnt that it was the idea of rebirth, as propounded in the *Gita* that kept India from making progress. I also learnt about the wonderful things the British did for my country. My rebuttal of these representations in *East Indians: Myths and Reality* was the beginning of my struggle as an anti-racist scholar.

I continue to teach and research in an academic environment that retains much of the arrogance displayed by the children in the school I visited. Its cultural and curricular practices militate against assigning more than a marginal space to non-Western, non-white cultures and societies. Such a skewered power relation with the dominant system makes me aware that I cannot do "disinterested," "objective" research that those in power loudly proclaim as proper "academic" research. I must fight politically, and in solidarity with other antiracist struggles to bring about admission equity, curriculum equity and employment equity on Canadian campuses. I hope my teaching, research, and political action will help to bring the day closer when universities will consider all cultures as equal and valuable and all human beings as equal and valuable.

3. The Vocabulary of the "Universal":
The Cultural Imperialism of the Universalist
Criteria of Western Literary Criticism

I feel that there is something being hidden by the terms "indigenous" and "metropolitan," or rather there is something not being
said. In my view, the real terms are "national democratic" cultures
and "imperialist" cultures, and the real tension is between the
national cultures of Africa—or the national cultures of Third World
peoples—and the imperialist cultures of Japan, Western Europe and
the United States.

NGUGI WA THIONG'O

Though Commonwealth literature can claim to have given rise to a
tremendous critical activity on the part of Western critics during the
last decade and a half, one would not be simplifying too much if one
were to say that much of this criticism boils down to a rather
repetitive discussion of two issues: the debt the works of the new
Commonwealth owe to the Western literary tradition and their
"universality." Indeed, the two issues seem to have divided the
Commonwealth family into two opposing camps which could be
defined as Western European versus Afro-Asian, the latter group
maintaining that the Western critics, instead of developing a sensitivity to other ways of apprehending the world, have simply imposed the traditional Western categories on the works from the new
Commonwealth, all in the name of "universality." In his "Thoughts
on the African Novel," Achebe describes this mentality as "the
dogma of universality." Taking issue with Eldred Jones's evalu-
ation of Soyinka whom Jones considers to be portraying "a universal problem" in *The Interpreters*, Achebe writes:

For supposing "events all over the world" have *not* shown "in

17

the new generation a similar dissatisfaction ... ," would it truly be invalid for a Nigerian writer seeing a dissatisfaction in *his* society to write about it? Am I being told, for Christ's sake, that before I write about any problem I must first verify whether they have it too in New York and London and Paris?[1]

In the statement, Achebe is denying validity to those interpretations which praise or criticize works on the basis of universality. Achebe is also denying the liberal humanist position that things in Nigeria must be the same as they are in New York, London and Paris since all human beings belong to the one big family called humanity. And finally, Achebe is denying another sacred liberal humanist assumption which believes that good literature concerns itself with universals, by claiming that he is going to address himself to the differences between Nigerians and the people residing in New York, London and Paris.

Achebe's views on these issues are by no means exceptional. Several Afro-Asian writers and critics have voiced objections against what has been considered Western cultural imperialism. Nevertheless, the universalist criteria continue to be used in Western literary criticism, and the users seem to imply high praise when they deem a Commonwealth writer to have universal appeal.

Though "universal" is a valorized term in the Western liberal humanist criticism, its use in the Afro-Asian context leads to certain misrepresentations and evasions. As Achebe's comments indicate, universalist criteria totally overlook the historical, time- and place-specific experience of a people in their insistence that life in Nigeria is more or less similar to life in the metropolitan centres of the Western world because of the essential brotherhood of man. The local and the specific are mere layers to the universalist critic underneath which can be discerned the archetypes of human drama. The following passage from an article published in a recent issue of *World Literature Written in English* is a good example of this type of criticism:

> [P]olitics is not the motivating force or central concern of his work. Naipaul recreates the political conflicts and tensions to be true to the ethos of the society he writes about and to create . . . a dramatic backdrop that serves to heighten his protago-

nists' personal conflicts and tensions. He does not make politics his exclusive thematic concern nor does he restrict himself to national issues. Naipaul's is a cosmopolitan, inter-nationalist consciousness, which surveys compassionately the human condition, not restrictively the political, the racial or the national.[2]

The author devalues the political, racial and national while valorizing the cosmopolitan and the international. Once he has established his hierarchies, he sets out to criticize writers (Achebe is named specifically) who write about the local politics as "publicists," and accuses them of "moral flabbiness."[3]

Thus, the universalist criteria are subtly selective: they prefer the writers who downplay the local and the specific as opposed to the writers engaged in portraying the day-to-day life of their societies as participants. Helen Tiffin comments that "an orthodoxy has developed which dismisses realist writers as inherently inferior to those with more overtly metaphysical interests."[4]

Such subtle selection and canon formation, with their political and ideological implications, confront a resistant reader in the majority of Western evaluations of Commonwealth writing. The following passage from Northrop Frye's "Across the River and Out of the Trees" is especially significant as it served as the theme for the 1984 conference of the Canadian Association of Commonwealth Languages and Literatures Studies:

> In an "instant world" of communication, there is no reason for cultural lag or for a difference between sophisticated writers in large centres and naive writers in smaller ones. A world like ours produces a single international style of which all existing literatures are regional developments. This international style is not a bag of rhetorical tricks but a way of seeing and thinking in a world controlled by uniform patterns of technology, and the regional development is a way of escaping from that uniformity. If we read, say, Wilson Harris's *Palace of the Peacock* and then Robert Kroetsch's *Badlands* one after the other, we find that there is no similarity between them, and that one story is steeped in Guyana and the other in Alberta. But certain structural affinities, such as the fold over in time, indicate that

they are both products of much the same phase of cultural development.[5]

The tone of the passage is very disturbing to me, a critic of new Commonwealth origins. For one thing, Frye seems to equate technological advance with literary evolution. The phrase "cultural lag" suggests a rather condescending attitude towards the traditional indigenous literatures. Then, we are not informed as to when this revolution in literature is supposed to have taken place. The causality is equally mysterious. Is the relatively new sophistication that Frye sees in the modern Third World literature a result of having learnt from the sophisticated writers of the metropolis or is it the result of the new "way of seeing and thinking" that is supposed to have come with the "uniform patterns of technology"? Obviously, Frye wants it both ways. For if Frye had attributed the sophistication of the "naive writers" solely to the influence of the "sophisticated writers," one could have validly objected that the hinterland society may not necessarily be sophisticated enough for comprehending the imported "international style." In order to ward off that objection, Frye claims that the "uniform patterns of technology" have brought societies around the world to the same level. Thus, one can say that if there are structural affinities in writers across the nations, they occur automatically, because of the similarity of life patterns brought about by technology.

It is clear to me that Frye's mental contortions and contradictions lead up to the same "universalist" approach that Achebe was protesting against. Achebe, and many others, reject Frye's claim that "uniform patterns of technology" have created a uniform world. As this discussion of the practice and pronouncements of several Indian and African writers will show, they assert that life in the Third World is different from life in London, Paris and New York. And they claim that the writer who writes about these differences has to create new forms for articulating these differences. Thus, while Frye believes in ready-made forms, or archetypes, a writer like Achebe believes that the local realities dictate their own structures.

However, Western critics have been so busy proving the universality of texts that they have had no time for dealing with the specificity of these texts. I would go further and state that the universalist categories of criticism have no means of dealing with the specificity of a text except in terms of setting or backdrop. The universalist methodology, in its exaggerated focus on form and character, neglects referentiality and context, thereby failing to assign inventiveness to writers who structure their works on those principles. The universalist critic, armed with his ready-made categories of narrative technique, symbolic patterns, motifs such as journey or quest, bildungsroman, pastoral, etc., overlooks the formal complexities that arise when a work openly or cryptically utilizes the collectively shared knowledge and experiences of a society: experience of colonialism, legends of heroes and villains, deeply held belief systems, rhetorical pronouncements of local elite such as politicians, businessmen and movie stars and so on. The universalist critic's lack of interest in the context also means that the fiercely political confrontations in works from the Third World are de-radicalized. The Western critical response to J P Clark's *The Raft* is a good example of this appropriation. As R N Egudu shows in his article, "J P Clark's *The Raft*: The Tragedy of Economic Impotence," the Western critics have totally overlooked Clark's emphasis on economic exploitation and read the play in existentialist terms, seeing it as an exploration of "the general plight of Man" set adrift in an indifferent universe.[6]

Such existentialist-universalist lamentations on "the human condition" can be heard over and over again in Western literary criticism and the same habits of discourse are carried over to the discussion of works from the new Commonwealth. The following remarks by Haydn Moore Williams on Jhabvala's work constitute a good example of the functions the "universal" performs:

> Jhabvala constantly stresses the universality of India's problems. Though institutions like the arranged marriage are traditionally Indian, many of the problems of the characters of Jhabvala's New Delhi could also be set in New York or London. . . . She gains this universality the more easily by concentrating on personal, amorous and marital themes within an acutely vivid observation of urban Indian society in the second half of the twentieth century.[7]

In this kind of analysis, the "universal" masks the refusal to see the unfamiliar and, perhaps, the uncomfortable. It helps Williams select "personal, amorous and marital themes" as the ones worth bothering about because they are the ones that can be understood anywhere. Earlier in the article Williams had commented that the central subject of Jhabvala's novels is "the theme of isolation, rebellion and reconciliation, and the problems of expatriation and adaptation to a foreign culture."[8] Once again, it is clear that the themes important to Williams are related to the private lives of individuals that never get tangled with the broad socio-political conflicts. Also, the implication is that conflicts can be solved at the individual level through individual action or through growth in maturity.

While this sort of critical approach may be applicable to the works emanating from the European tradition, it is inadequate for judging the works by the writers from the new Commonwealth for the simple reason that it remains silent about institutional exploitation, caste and class domination, and economic and political neocolonialism, issues which cannot be resolved at the individual level through a personal growth in maturity. These are the factors that make life in Nigeria or India different from life in London, New York and Paris, and novels from the new Commonwealth countries can claim to be different because they treat the lives of their characters not as isolated individuals going on actual or spiritual journeys and finding their own individual resolutions, but as individuals moulded, confronted, and interfered with by their social environment at every step in their lives.

The Western critic, his sensibility trained by the forms of Western literature in which the individual has long held the centre of the stage, is unable to do justice to those works from the new Commonwealth in which community life and larger socio-political issues are of central importance.[9] When the Western critic applies the categories of character development, psychological verisimilitude, individual relationships such as love and marriage, and individual confrontation of problems of existence to these works, he performs an act of violence. A very good example of this kind of violence is the UNESCO English translation of the Bengali classic *Pather Panchali*. The translators, claiming that the "naive genius " of Bibhuti Bhusan Bandopadhyaya was not familiar with the requirements of the novel form, chopped off about seventy-five pages from the text:

In spite of its episodic structure and its occasional abrupt transitions from one incident to another, it is emotionally coherent, and its narrative is integrated about the children in their village. Yet it would appear that the author achieved this coherence, this dramatic unity, without fully realizing that he had done so; for having brought the story to a point of climax he does not end, but continues with chapters which emotionally and dramatically belong to the sequel. . . .

With these considerations in mind we have ended *Pather Panchali* with Opu looking out of the train window sobbing his goodbyes to his sister, his home and his village.[10]

One can only hope that no other works from the Third World have been mangled in this arbitrary, ethnocentric fashion. What the translators consider to be "episodic," "abrupt," and "anticlimactic" seems so only if we think that the novel's main preoccupation is a character named Opu. The fact that the writer did not think so is ascertained by his title which refers to an oral art form of Bengal. The writer's choice to structure his work in the loose episodic manner of a *Panchali,* and to adopt the narrative persona of a *Panchali* singer is motivated by his need to go beyond the novelistic conventions of the West which have no provisions for addressing a group audience. What Bandopadhyaya wanted most was to portray a vanishing mode of life and when he chose a form which was also vanishing, he further intensified the sense of loss he wanted his readers familiar with the *Panchali* and its itinerant singers to feel. If we assume that the village of Nishchindipur, and not Opu, is the focus of the novel, we will come to appreciate the relevance of the section the UNESCO edition purged out. The last section describes the life of Opu's family in the city and how the city finally destroys the family. The novel's conclusion with the *Panchali* singer-narrator's sardonic comments on Opu's intense longing to go back to Nishchindipur has an inevitability that is quite obvious to the reader familiar with the indigenous form employed by the novelist.

As works like *Pather Panchali*, Prem Chand's *Godan*, Raja Rao's *Kanthapura*, and Salman Rushdie's *Midnight's Children* show, the Indian novelist often creates forms which are markedly different from the fiction which is structured around a central hero figure. All of these novels are crowded with characters who may be considered extraneous if one went by the conventions of a main plot and central characters. However, if one chose to read these novels as exploration of community life and its historic transformations, every thing seems to fall in its place. Instead of drawing Jamesian "portraits" of sensitive individuals, this type of novel attempts to project a vision of the individual within the community, the individual under the sway of large movements of history.[11]

It was an interesting revelation for me to read Chinua Achebe's claim that his contribution to the novel form was his "emphasis on the community, as opposed to the individual."[12] He reinforced my own conclusion that the individual-centred forms of Western literature did not display that richness of community life I had experienced in the works of major Indian and African novelists. His statement supported my belief that the decentring of the individual protagonist was the main difference between the Western and the Indian and African novel and that this decentring was related to our different notions about the individual.

Raymond Williams has commented that the disappearance of a recognizable social community has been the bane of the English novel and that the great works of the nineteenth and the early twentieth century are mournings for that lost community life. Rather than attempting to recreate a community, the novelists, Williams says, surrendered to the forces that were fragmenting it. Interestingly enough, what Williams would like to see in the English novel is quite similar to what does happen in the novels of writers like Achebe, Ngugi, Raja Rao and Rushdie:

> Not selected persons, not persons composed in a single life's trajectory or around an idea or a theme; but there in the way neighbours are, friends are, the people we work with are. . . .
> And it's one of the paradoxes of the literature of developed individualism that in a later mode this is never really so; never so for others.[13]

I believe that the conventions of the individual-centred forms make it possible for the Western novelists to escape from directly confronting the burning social issues of their times. Issues such as the enclosure movement and the uprooting of rural population, industrial unrest, Chartism, colonization and women's rights got treated only as adjuncts to the main plot that inevitably concerned itself with a man-woman relationship. In a recent feminist study called *Victims of Convention,* Jean E Kennard has proposed something similar. She believes that a large number of Victorian as well as modern novelists have been unable to explore women's problems because they felt compelled to structure their novels according to the two suitor convention whereby a young woman is educated by the process of having to choose between two male suitors: one good and intelligent and the other evil.[14] While one may not totally agree with her diagnosis, the fact remains that the triangle has been a staple device in the Western novel. The group-based Western novels such as George Gissing's *The Odd Women* and Marilyn French's *The Women's Room* are an exception to this norm.

The writers in the new Commonwealth countries have had to reject the individual-centred novel as it does not reflect the important role of kinship relationships in the cultures of their countries. The custom of arranged marriage, for example, makes it virtually impossible for the Indian novelist to use the great theme of courtship and marriage, unless in a parodic way. As R K Narayan says, "The eternal triangle, such a standby for the Western writer, is worthless as a theme for an Indian, our social circumstances not providing adequate facilities for the eternal triangle."[15] The novelist, then, has to construct new structures which will articulate the indigenous reality. These structures have to be different because the Indian or African experience of selfhood is different. For example, while Western literature and philosophy have emphasized the primacy of the individual, Indian literature and tradition have laid emphasis on the primacy of the family and the community. In the Indian context, the well-being of the individual is often tied to the well-being of the larger group to which he or she belongs.

The new Commonwealth novelists, then, have had to build structures which will allow them to capture the spider-web of relationships which constitute community life in the developing countries. These structures may seem loose or episodic to the Western critic, yet they have a coherence if judged in accordance with the forms of experience they set out to explore. These structures are political choices on the part of the new Commonwealth writers, a declaration that the metropolitan forms do not fit their needs. However, the innovations and experimentations of these writers have often gone unnoticed. Their use of parabolic structures, indigenous storytelling conventions, folk tales, parodies of Western and indigenous forms and rituals, have not attracted adequate attention due to the critics' obsession with Western categories. As J P Clark complained, the Third World writers are discussed as though they did not have "two hands"—one European and one homegrown—but only one.[16]

Contrary to the assertions of the liberal humanist critics, literary appreciation as well as literary production are culture based and no universal criteria can be worked out that will apply regardless of cultural differences. It is not possible to accept that the quest, the Jungian journey to the underworld, the individual's growth from ignorance to knowledge, etc., are "universal" archetypes. These are the forms created by a civilization whose physical frontiers have continually expanded during the last four centuries. For example, instead of the quest, the main motif of Indian epics is exile. The characters of the *Ramayana* and the *Mahabharata* go to the forest against their will, in obedience to the command of the parents in the first one and as punishment for having lost at gambling in the second. Similarly, in Achebe's *Things Fall Apart*, exile from his tribal village is the greatest misfortune that befalls Okonkwo, second only to the disruption of the tribal pattern of life by the arrival of the colonizer.

The journey is a form suitable to the outsider and that is the way Conrad and Patrick White have used it in *Heart of Darkness* and *A Fringe of Leaves*. However, if one wants to explore the destruction of communities, as it appears to an insider, the quest will not do. Yet, our reverence for metropolitan opinions is so great that we cannot see without the lenses provided by our Western training. In a paper on Arun Kolatkar's *Jejuri*, S K Desai comments on the "Westernized critical sensibility" of Indian critics that "has been quick to find in *Jejuri* a characteristic quest-poem or an odyssey-spiritual or anti-spiritual."[17] Similarly, Meenakshi Mukherjee, in a paper entitled "Macaulay's Imperishable Empire," laments the Indian critics' inability to think on their own. "Their slavish attitude," she says, "makes it possible for a string of quotations from the latest Western critics and a recitation of the current Western literary jargon to be called literary criticism."[18]

S.K. Desai

Desai pleads for what he calls "cultural inwardness." He wants the Western critics to familiarize themselves with the culture before they comment on its literature. He also finds fault with the lack of awareness on the part of Western critics about what is being said about indigenous literary works by the native critics and readers.

However, though Commonwealth literature is now taught in several Canadian universities, few of them subscribe to Indian or African journals. I feel that the majority of the Western critics are too simplistic in their response to the works of the new Commonwealth because they haven't bothered to familiarize themselves with the cultures from which these works have sprung. Therefore, they are unable to see these literary works in their relationship with the other discourses that go on in the society which produced them. As Fredric Jameson suggests, cultural artifacts have a "relational place in a dialogical system,"[19] and the work of the critic should be to bring out their relational nature. For example, literary works often use mythic structures, quotations of political, religious and business leaders, folk and scriptural wisdom, collectively revered cultural attitudes, and past literary works as sub-texts. The Western critics, however, remain tone deaf to these nuances that make all the difference in interpretation. Instead, they concentrate on the characters and events and "universalize" them. Take, for example, these remarks of S C Harrex on R K Narayan:

> Narayan's world abounds with images of turbulence, with "harassments and distractions" and labyrinthine approaches to human relationships. Man is constantly harassed by officialdom, red tape, bureaucracy; by the aggressive trigger-happy type . . . or the supercilious western-educated enemy of tradition, or even the child armed with a catapult and sadistic urges.[20]

"Man" here stands for the whole of humanity, obviously. The word obscures for the user, as well as the reader, the divisions in a society. "Man is constantly harassed by officialdom" glosses over the fact that officialdom is quite selective in its behaviour. Nor does such identificatory terminology identify the causes of things and actions. They seem to happen mysteriously and for no apparent reason.

The "universalists" forget the relational place of the work that

Jameson was talking about. They forget that literary works are polemical, and that their polemicity can only be understood by taking their context into account. The "universalists" ignore these considerations when they talk about "Man." As far as critical responses to Indo-Anglian literature are concerned, for example, everything boils down to clichés such as Western rationality and Eastern spirituality. Thus, Kamala Markandaya's *A Silence of Desire* is reduced to a schematic reconciliation of the East-West conflict in Indian society. In such critiques, Dandekar stands for the Western rational attitudes while his wife, Sarojini, symbolizes the spiritual East.[21] However, I see Dandekar as an individual caught in a great chain of hierarchy, oppressing those beneath him and oppressed by those above him. The hierarchy is symbolized by the eight-story tenement building Dandekar lives in and his progress in the hierarchy is traced through his gradual moves from the topmost floor to the ground floor. As a clerk, he epitomizes India's lower middle class, domineering with those below and submissive to the ones above. That this hierarchical nature of his relationships is the main issue of the novel becomes evident when Dandekar, after having been warned by his new superior, wonders whether he has not related to Sarojini as a boss all their married life. His symbolic value as a representative of the Western way of life is further undercut by his fear of Western films and the Western notions of marriage. Dandekar does not want the hierarchical nature of his marriage to change and is frightened by what he sees as his wife's yearning for independence.

A Silence of Desire is much more than an abstract, mental anguish over the clash between Western rationality and Eastern spirituality, so-called. It is a concrete exploration of the realities of lower-middle-class Indian life at the bureaucratic, matrimonial and economic levels. To restrict the novel to a simple theorem of East meets West is to trivialize it.

Such trivialization will continue to occur until the foreign critic acquires "cultural inwardness." To ignore the social context, i.e. the writer's dialogical relationship with his society, and to superimpose categories that claim to be beyond the restraints of specificity is to falsify and deradicalize the literary works of the new Commonwealth. In the neocolonial situation, when the dictates of the metropolis determine what will be said, thought, written and read in the peripheries, we from the new Commonwealth face the danger of becoming alienated from our own realities. As C D Narsimaiyah says, our own critical faculties have been reduced to "catching up with other people's yesterdays."[22] Given the imperatives of the present-day imperialistic world order, the Western critic must ask himself if he is not, per chance, playing the role of a cultural imperialist when he resorts to "universalist" criteria.

4. Ideology in the Classroom:

A Case Study in the Teaching of English

Literature in Canadian Universities

This paper was written in order to articulate the sense of personal anguish and alienation that I feel as a teacher of literature whose sex, race and birth in a newly independent Asian country set her constantly at odds with the consensus that appears to reign in the departments of English across Canadian universities. The terms of this consensus, it seems to me, are not so very different from the ones prevailing in American universities as demonstrated, for example, by Richard Ohmann in his *English in America*.

Generally speaking, we, the Canadian university teachers of English, do not consider issues of the classroom worth critical scrutiny. Indeed, there is hardly any connection between our pedagogy and our scholarly research. A new teacher, looking for effective teaching strategies, will discover to her utter dismay that no amount of reading of scholarly publications will be of any help when she faces a class of undergraduates. In fact, the two discourses—those of pedagogy and scholarly research—are diametrically opposed and woe betide the novice who uses the language of current scholarly discourse in the classroom.

As an outsider, it has never ceased to amaze me that Canadian literary scholars do not seem perturbed by this doublespeak. Not having the same skills myself, I gape with open mouth at my colleagues who switch so easily from one to another. Perhaps, blessed with what Keats called "Negative Capability," they are able to hold two completely contradictory systems of thought in suspension.

Edward Said, in his essay in *The Politics of Interpretation*, says that the "mission of the humanities" in contemporary American society is "to represent *noninterference* in the affairs of the everyday world."[1] He charges the American practitioners of the humanities with concealing, atomizing, depoliticizing and mystifying the "unhumanistic process" that informs the *laissez faire* society of what he calls "Reaganism." The classroom experience I narrate in this paper concretized for me the ahistorical realm in which American and, yes, Canadian, university teachers of literature ply their trade.

What I have recounted here is not unique at all and I continue to come across student papers that share the innocence about history I describe in this paper. However, this particular experience was a watershed in my personal history since it allowed me, for the first time, to articulate to myself the lineaments of my disagreement with the dominant academic discourses.

The case study presented here is taken from the period 1983-84, when I was teaching at the University of Regina, Saskatchewan. A large part of the teaching done at the Department of English of that university consists of English 100: Introduction to Literature. It is a compulsory course whereby the professors of English supposedly infuse first-year students with a love of literature. Since the aim of the course is to acquaint students with prominent literary genres, almost all teachers of the course use anthologies that contain short stories, poems and, at times, plays and novels as well. Quite often, the anthologies are American.

The short fiction anthology I used for my introductory English 100 class—I deliberately chose a Canadian one—includes a short story by Margaret Laurence entitled "The Perfume Sea."[2] This story, as I interpret it, underlines the economic and cultural domination of the Third World. However, even though I presented this interpretation of the story to my students in some detail, they did not even consider it when they wrote their essays. While the story had obviously appealed to them—almost forty percent chose to write on it—they ignored the political meaning entirely.

I was thoroughly disappointed by my students' total disregard for local realities treated in the short story. Nevertheless, their papers did give me an understanding of how their education had allowed them to neutralize the subversive meanings implicit in a piece of good literature, such as the Laurence story.

The story, from my point of view, is quite forthright in its purpose. Its locale is Ghana on the eve of independence from British

31

rule. The colonial administrators are leaving and this has caused financial difficulties for Mr Archipelago and Doree who operate the only beauty parlour within a radius of one hundred miles around an unnamed small town. Though the equipment is antiquated, and the parlour operators not much to their liking, the ladies have put up with it for want of a better alternative.

With the white clientele gone, Mr Archipelago and Doree have no customers left. The parlour lies empty for weeks until one day the crunch comes in the shape of their Ghanaian landlord, Mr Tachie, demanding rent. Things, however, take an upturn when Mr Archipelago learns that Mr Tachie's daughter wants to look like a "city girl" and constantly pesters her father for money to buy shoes, clothes and make-up. Mr Archipelago, in a flash of inspiration, discovers that Mercy Tachie is the new consumer to whom he can sell his "product": "Mr Tachie, you are a bringer of miracles! . . . There it was, all the time, and we did not see it. We, even we, Doree, will make history—you will see."[3] The claim about making history is repeated twice in the story and is significantly linked to the history made by Columbus. For Mr Archipelago is very proud of the fact that he was born in Genoa, Columbus's home town. The unpleasant aspect of this act of making history is unmistakably spelt out: "He [Columbus] was once in West Africa, you know, as a young seaman, at one of the old slave-castles not far from here. And he, also, came from Genoa."[4]

The symbolic significance of the parlour is made quite apparent from the detailed attention Laurence gives to its transformation. While the pre-independence sign had said:

ARCHIPELAGO
English-Style Barber
European Ladies' Hairdresser (p. 211)

the new sign says:

ARCHIPELAGO & DOREE
Barbershop
All-Beauty Salon
African Ladies A Speciality (p. 221)

With the help of a loan from Mr Tachie, the proprietors install hair-straightening equipment and buy shades of makeup suitable for the African skin. However, though the African ladies show much interest from a distance, none of them enters the shop. Two weeks later, Mercy Tachie hesitantly walks into the salon "because if you are having no customers, he [Mr Tachie] will never be getting his money from you" (p. 222). Mercy undergoes a complete transformation in the salon and comes out looking like a "city girl," the kind she has seen in *Drum* magazine. Thus, Mr Archipelago and Doree are "saved" by "an act of Mercy" (p. 226). They have found a new role in the life of this newly independent country: to help the African bourgeoisie slavishly imitate the values of its former colonial masters.

These political overtones are reinforced by the overall poverty the story describes and the symbolic linking of the white salon operators with the only black merchant in town. The division between his daughter and other African women who go barefoot with babies on their backs further indicates the divisive nature of the European implant. Other indications of the writer's purpose are apparent from her caricature of Mr Archipelago and Doree, a device which prevents emotional identification with them. The fact that both of them have no known national identities—both of them keep changing their stories—is also significant, for it seems to say that, like Kurtz in *Heart of Darkness*, they represent the whole white civilization. The story thus underplays the lives of individuals in order to emphasize these larger issues: the nature of colonialism as well as its aftermath when the native elite takes over without really changing the colonial institutions except for their names.

This, then, was the aspect of the story in which I was most interested, no doubt because I am myself from a former colony of the Raj. During class discussions, I asked the students about the symbolic significance of the hair straightening equipment, the change of names, the identification of Mr Archipelago with Columbus, *Drum* magazine, and the characters of Mr Tachie and Mercy Tachie.

However, the students based their essays not on these aspects, but on how "believable" or "likeable" the two major characters in the story were, and how they found happiness in the end by accepting change. That is to say, the two characters were freed entirely from the restraints of the context, i.e., the colonial situation, and evaluated solely on the basis of their emotional relationship with each other. The outer world of political turmoil, the scrupulously observed class system of the colonials, the contrasts between wealth and poverty, were nonexistent in their papers. As one student put it, the conclusion of the story was "The perfect couple walking off into the sunset, each happy that they had found what had eluded both of them all their lives, companionship and privacy all rolled into one relationship." For another, they symbolized "the anxiety and hope of humanity . . . the common problem of facing or not facing reality."

I was astounded by my students' ability to close themselves off to the disturbing implications of my interpretation and devote their attention to expatiating upon "the anxiety and hope of humanity," and other such generalizations as change, people, values, reality, etc. I realized that these generalizations were ideological. They enabled my students to efface the differences between British bureaucrats and British traders, between colonizing whites and colonized blacks, and between rich blacks and poor blacks. They enabled them to believe that all human beings faced dilemmas similar to the ones faced by the two main characters in the story.

Though, thanks to Kenneth Burke, I knew the rhetorical subterfuges which generalizations like "humanity" imply, the papers of my students made me painfully aware of their ideological purposes. I saw that they help us to translate the world into our own idiom by erasing the ambiguities and the unpleasant truths that lie in the crevices. They make us oblivious to the fact that society is not a homogeneous grouping but an assortment of groups where we belong to one particular set called " us," as opposed to the other set or sets we distinguish as "them."

The most painful revelation came when I recognized the source of my students' vocabulary. Their analysis, I realized, was in the time-honoured tradition of that variety of criticism which presents literary works as "universal." The test of a great work of literature, according to this tradition, is that despite its particularity, it speaks to all times and all people. As Brent Harold notes, "It is a rare discussion of literature that does not depend heavily on the universal 'we' (meaning we human beings), on 'the human condition,' 'the plight of modern man,' 'absurd man' and other convenient abstractions which obscure from their users the specific social basis of their own thought......"[5]

Thus, all conflict eliminated with the help of the universal "we," what do we have left but the "feelings" and "experiences" of individual characters? The questions in the anthologies reflect that. When they are not based on matters of technique—where one can short circuit such problems entirely—they ask students whether such and such character deserves our sympathy, or whether such and such a character undergoes change, or, in other words, an initiation. As Richard Ohmann comments:

> The student focuses on a character, on the poet's attitude, on the individual's struggle towards understanding—but rarely, if ever, on the social forces that are revealed in every dramatic scene and almost every stretch of narration in fiction. Power, class, culture, social order and disorder—these staples of literature are quite excluded from consideration in the analytic tasks set for Advanced Placement candidates.[6]

Instead of facing up to the realities of "power, class, culture, social order and disorder," literary critics and editors of literature anthologies hide behind the universalist vocabulary that only mystifies the true nature of reality. For example, the editorial introduction to "The Perfume Sea" considers the story in terms of categories that are supposedly universal and eternal:

> Here is a crucial moment in human history seen from inside a beauty parlour and realized in terms of the "permanent wave." But while feminine vanity is presented as the only changeless element in a world of change, Mrs Laurence, for all her lightness of touch, is not "making fun" of her Africans or Europeans. In reading the story, probe for the deeper layers of human anxiety and hope beneath the comic surfaces. (p. 201)

Though the importance of "a crucial moment in history" is acknowledged here, it is only to point out the supposedly changeless: that highly elusive thing called "feminine vanity." The term performs the function of achieving the desired identification between all white women and all black women, regardless of the barriers of race and class. The command to probe "the deeper layers of human anxiety and hope"—a command that my students took more seriously than their teacher's alternative interpretation—works to effectively eliminate consideration of disturbing socio-political realities.

This process results in the promotion of what Ohmann calls the "prophylactic view of literature" (p. 63). Even the most provocative literary work, when seen from such a perspective, is emptied of its subversive content. After such treatment, as Ohmann puts it, "It will not cause any trouble for the people who run schools or colleges, for the military-industrial complex, for anyone who holds power. It can only perpetuate the misery of those who don't" (p. 61).

The editor-critic thus functions as the castrator. He makes sure that the young minds will not get any understanding of how our society actually functions and how literature plays a role in it. Instead of explaining these relationships, the editor-critic feeds students on a vocabulary that pretends that human beings and their institutions have not changed a bit during the course of history, that they all face the same problems as human beings. Thus, another anthology used by several of my colleagues divides its subject-matter into four groups called "Innocence and Experience," "Conformity and Rebellion," "Love and Hate" and "The Presence of Death." The Preface justifies the classification thus: "The arrangement of the works in four thematic groups provides opportunities to explore diverse attitudes towards the same powerful human tendencies and experiences and to contrast formal treatment as well."[7]

The problem is that it is the editors' fiat that has decided what the "powerful human tendencies" are and how they should be treated. The introductions to the four sections talk about "the protagonist" and "tendencies" in a language that conveys to me that literature is about initiation and loss of innocence, about the lone rebel fighting against such authoritarian agencies as the state and society, about love and hate between men and women, and, about the inevitability of death. Literature, according to this line of thinking, is obviously not about the problems of oppression and injustice, about how to create a just society, about how to understand one's situation in society and to do something about it. Literature does not speak about people as social beings, as members of political or social alliances that they have voluntarily chosen.

I would not like to act naive and ask, like Barbara Kessel: "Why is it impossible for liberal critics to conceive of miserable, oppressed people freely choosing to struggle against their own oppression?"[8] The reason is that it is far more comfortable to hide behind a vocabulary which, on the one hand, overlooks one's own privileged position and, on the other, makes everyone look equally privileged. It creates, in the imagination of the user, a society "free, classless, urbane," by lifting the work of art from "the bondage of history."[9] And if, my students, who come mainly from the privileged section of an overall affluent society, perform the same sleight-of-hand, why should I feel unduly disturbed? After all, as Auden says, "Poetry makes nothing happen." The only remaining question, then, is what am I doing in that classroom?

Terry Eagleton says that "explanation and interpretation 'come to an end' . . . when we arrive at a certain interpretative logjam or sticking-place and recognize that we shall not get any further until we transform the practical forms of life in which our interpretations are inscribed."[10] He makes me realize that I can't fight a quixotic battle in the classroom for historicity and politicization. In fact, I have at times been accused by some of my outraged students of "bringing politics into a literature class." In a similar vein, a very well-respected Canadian scholar in my field intimated to me that my research was "old-fashioned," i.e. "sociological," and that if I wanted to consolidate my precarious foothold in academia, I should think about doing some "fashionable" research, i.e. "semiotics," "deconstruction," "feminism," and so on. (I found it interesting that feminism to him was only another "fashion.")

My feeling is that the transformation of the practical forms of life which Eagleton speaks of is not around the corner in Canada. Those on the margin face an uphill task in terms of sheer physical and moral survival in the system. Once accepted, they face the prospect of being typecast as the "token black," or the "token ethnic," or the "token feminist." Their "diversion," then, becomes a nice variation in the vast edifice of cultural reproduction that goes on in departments of literature and literary journals.

Said talks about the need for a "fully articulated program of interference" (p. 31). This paper is a partial attempt in that direction. I have hoped to generate a debate over issues that are very important to me as a teacher and a non-white woman from the Third World.

I am glad, let me add, that this paper has finally found an audience. It was submitted in an earlier version to the "Literature and Ideology" category of the annual conference of the Association of Canadian University Teachers of English (ACUTE) held at Guelph in 1984. While ACUTE may have turned down this submission for reasons other than ideological, what I found really disturbing was the total lack of attention to pedagogical issues in the conference programme. After all, the bulk of our jobs are provided by first-year English courses and the communication strategies we adopt in our classrooms should therefore be an important part of our discussions when we meet for our annual conference, and it should be recognized that the responses of our students constitute an important mirror both of our performance and of our values. It does not behoove us as scholars to be oblivious to the social repercussions of our activities in the classroom.

If one looks at the 1984 ACUTE conference program, one gets the impression that the only officially sanctioned valid response to literary works is structuralist-formalist. The following topics are representative of the kind of fare conference participants were treated to: "Sedulous Aping?: Redefining Parody Today," "John Webster's Jacobean Experiments in Dramatic Mimesis," "What Does It Mean To Imitate an Action?" "Whalley on Mimesis and Tragedy," "Interruption in *The Tempest*" and so on. Even the "Literature and Ideology" category was appropriated for formalistic preoccupations: the two papers in this section were entitled "Christianity as Ideology in Rudy Wiebe's *The Scorched-Wood People*" and "Dickens' Good Women: An Analysis of the Influence of Social Ideology on Literary Form."

Surely, literature is more than form? What about the questions regarding the ideology and social class of a writer, the role and ideology of the patrons and disseminators of literature, the role of literature as a social institution and, finally, the role of the teacher-critic as a transmitter of dominant social and cultural values? Have these questions no place in our professional deliberations?

5. The Third World in the Dominant Western Cinema: Responses of a Third World Viewer

Recent feminist criticism of dominant cinema has shown how it constructs images of women to suit the psychological needs of the male spectator and the male filmmaker. The woman is contained, co-opted, and often dismembered so that the male needs of dominance and status quo can be satisfied. The feminists insist that what we see on the screen are male fantasies of what a woman ought to be. The cinema cleverly displaces the conflicts of male-female relations in the real world and contains the intransigent woman through its narrative and cinematic techniques. Sometimes it succeeds so well that the female spectator gives her allegiance to it.[1]

As a female viewer, I have no difficulty in sympathizing with the analysis of the Western feminists. However, as a Third World viewer, occupying a marginal space in places like the media and the universities, I have other concerns which I consider to be more wide-ranging. My concerns are with the misrepresentation, manipulation and fantasization of the people of the Third World. It is not only my gender that the Western films demean, but my culture, history and racial being as well—if the individualistic West can understand such a thing as the collective being.

Of late there has been a spate of films, television serials, songs and novels about the Third World. They join in with the images of the starving, the sick and the dying whom the likes of Mother Teresa administer. One needs also to add to these images the voices of people like Ronald Reagan and George Schultz who tell the naughty, socialist-minded Third World leaders that they will never be able to raise their countries above the dung heap if they don't adopt capitalistic ways.

What is, of course, hidden behind these images and pronouncements is the bitter history of colonialism. However, what is not admitted does not go away but keeps hovering like Banquo's ghost at the banquet. No matter how many fathoms deep the white man tries to bury his burden, it continues to come unrepressed. Or else, why make films like *A Passage to India, The Gods Must Be Crazy, Out of Africa* and *Crocodile Dundee?*

Of course, there is nothing wrong with facing one's past and coming to terms with it. If one does it honestly, one can lay to rest the nagging anguish caused by the sins of omission and commission, and get on with the business of living. To a certain extent, that does happen in *Gandhi.* It is an honest movie which takes an unflinching look at the past. Whatever its shortcomings, it is a film that continues to attract me and retains its appeal through multiple viewings. It is because I feel that the filmmaker respected the country and the people he was portraying and allowed them to speak in their own voice.

This is not what one can say about *A Passage to India, Out of Africa* and *The Gods Must Be Crazy.* What I see happening in these is the white man's attempt to exorcize the past and to make it appear as though the bad part—the sin and guilt part—never happened. What I see happening in these films is cultural recolonization, an attempt to go back to the place of one's past crime and recreate the past in a way that the crime is displaced, muffled, washed out.

That impulse, of course, is there in much of the white man's literature. The question is, how to do what has to be done and stop the naggings of the guilt-ridden conscience? In James Fennimore Cooper's novel, *Deerslayer*, Natty Bumpo, the good white man, kills an Indian in self-defence, and the dying Indian utters a benediction absolving Bumpo of the guilt. As Peter Abrahams has David Brown, the black pastor, say in *The View from Coyaba*: "It is not enough to take what is mine. You want me to tell you it is right for you to do it."[2]

That is what happens in all the three films I want to look at. The white man in them wants the Third World native to tell him that it was all right for him to have taken away the victim's birthright, that it was indeed good for the native that the white man came to his country and "civilized" him. And if the Third World native refuses to do it in the real world—just look at the voting records of Third World countries in the UN—the white man will construct images of him in the imaginary world of art and make him perform the desired genuflections.

These films use many subtle and not so subtle techniques of cinematic discourse to present an aesthetic experience that is demeaning and infuriating for the Third World viewer. These devices include distortions of history and contemporary reality, subtle omissions, imposition of the perennial Western form of romance, caricature of the native peoples' viewpoints and characters, exoticization of their land, and presentation of Western characters as larger than life and benevolent educators. Most Westerners do not see the racist and imperialist designs of these aesthetic experiences. As well, they dismiss the Third World viewer's responses as "ideological" and "too political," art supposedly being free from ideology and politics.

A Passage to India, for example, was lauded whole-heartedly in the media as another of David Lean's classics and awarded its share of Oscars. Most of my white friends commented on how beautiful the photography was, how lovely the Indian landscapes. Of course, there were a few deviations from the Forster novel, but then the filmmaker is allowed to take a few liberties, they said. The more astute among them reacted negatively to the clown-like portrayal of Professor Godbole and the happy ending where Aziz bids farewell to his white friends in the most submissive manner. But the portrayal of the Third World is not a matter of identity crisis for them as it is to us, products of the soil, visible carriers of its stamp upon our skins, our features, our minds. They went back to teaching the canonical works of English and American literature, popular literature being a pariah at our universities, along with questions of racism and imperialism.

One cannot go back to these higher pursuits, however, if one has a child who must go to see films like *Gods Must Be Crazy* and *Crocodile Dundee* because all his other classmates have seen them. One must sit through the films, feeling like a spoilsport and a weirdo, because everyone else seems to be laughing their heads off. And, finally, one must go through an impassioned session of discussions with a nine-year-old, making him aware of the indignities perpetrated on his kind of people in the name of harmless fun. One feels a sense of profound alienation at such times. One writes to counter that alienation and to put on record that the discourse of cultural imperialism is not the only discourse.

What, then, bothers one most? Perhaps it is the all-pervasive narrative structure of a white man loving a white woman in an exotic tropical landscape filled with equally exotic natives. The centre of all the three films is this romance, embellished with strains of classical Western music. What is at a premium is the sexuality of the white characters. It is explored hauntingly. The cinematic experience is entirely devoted to the tensions of heterosexual romance. All else is secondary.

Thus, in *A Passage to India,* Lean shifts the focus away from Dr Aziz, who is the true hero of the Forster novel, and turns it on Adela. The film opens with her. Lean manufactures a rather tacky section in which Adela sees erotic sculptures in the wilderness, supposedly "to let you see that she is beginning to awaken sexually . . . because India can do this, you know."[3] The section subtly changes and depoliticizes the toughest aspects of Forster's novel. In the film, Adela is overpowered by this erotic awakening to such an extent that she dares to talk to Aziz about "love" and asks him whether he "loved" his wife. His reply to this is, "We were young, and we were a man and a woman." In the book, however, the conversation is not so civilized. Instead of talking about "love," Adela asks Dr Aziz: "Have you one wife or more than one?"[4] It is this insensitive question that leads to disaster and not Adela's sexual awakening. Stung, muttering, "Damn the English even at their best," Aziz plunges into one of the caves "to recover his balance."[5]

The film, however, sweetens the imperialistic relations of the British and the Indians to mere social misunderstanding. The "bridge party" is seen as a personal failure of the Turtons who just happen to be bad-mannered. Mrs Moore's acid comments about "an exercise in power and the subtle pleasures of personal superiority" somehow make it all right to have an empire if only one exercised good manners. The book is much tougher on Mrs Moore.

The "love" talk helps Lean to rewrite the court scene in an idiom as tacky as the fake erotic sculptures. Lean tells us that Ronny has willingly stepped down as magistrate in Das's favour because of the stringent requirements of British justice and sense of fair play and not because, as the novel has it, the Indian defence lawyers have demanded it. Finally, there is a long, awkward statement from Adela about her "intimate" conversation with Aziz about "love" and how she came to realize that she and Ronny did not love each other. It is Adela's sexuality, her Western cultural values about love as essential for marriage that gain the centre of the stage, obliterating her insensitive assault on Aziz's sensibility.

Focusing the film on Adela's sexual misadventure allows Lean to decentre Dr Aziz. How does it matter to him if Aziz is the first character to whom we are introduced in the novel, or that the book also closes with him, aloof and intransigent? The Aziz we meet in the film is a wimp and not one who, "like all Indians," is "skilful in the slighter impertinences."[6] Thus, in the book, when Mrs Turton and Mrs Lesley appropriate Aziz's tonga without even noticing him, let alone asking him, he subtly, ironically underscores their rudeness by commenting: "You are most welcome, ladies."[7] The film allows no such "impertinences." This attitude is what, probably, made Victor Bannerjee, the Indian movie actor playing Aziz, comment bitterly on the Hollywoodian imperatives of the film.

One of the major final let downs of the film comes when we see Fielding and Stella projected against the Himalayas with loud background music and a submissive Aziz bidding them goodbye. The novel admitted that power relationships cannot be transformed into friendships. The film papers over this profound statement in a most awkward and disturbing manner. What else can one expect from a producer-director who believes in the white man's burden? Lean comments in an interview that he deliberately "toned down" the novel's hatred towards the British Raj. "It's all very well to criticize the English but just take a look at New Delhi, look at the railway system, look at the postal system—which works. We've left them all sorts of bad things, I suppose, but they also got some very good things."[8]

Not only does Aziz embrace Fielding, unlike the bitter and vitriolic Aziz of the novel, we hear his voice reading a conciliatory letter to Adela asking her to "forgive him." It is a very subtle manipulation of the semihumorous, semi-ironic letter he writes in the novel. Of course, he never asks her to "forgive him." Nor does he say: "It has taken me all this time for me to appreciate your courage." The poor native, it took him two years to learn his manners. The film ends with Adela back in England, standing against a window, as the rain falls soothingly outside. As Michael Sragow so approvingly puts it: "It's as if, with its wild panoramic beauty and apocalyptic catastrophes, her time in India was a primal dream—a dream she now carries with her, every waking hour."[9]

What a nice closure! The native is put where he belongs—in the "primal dream" that comes to disturb one's tranquillity once in a while. One can continue with the business of daily living once one has contained the native in this dream space. In fact, it is a double containment. The native is relegated to the subordinate role in the dream structure of the film and then further relegated to the dim memory of the white character gone back to the metropolis.

At least this is what a Third World viewer sees in films like *Gods Must Be Crazy*, *Out of Africa* and *Crocodile Dundee*. The native in all these films is the white man's fantasy of the noble savage, naked and painted, content in his habitat. Mick Dundee of *Crocodile Dundee* is the fantasy white man who lives in harmony with nature and is at home with the natives. He even paints his face and participates in the ritual midnight dance in the recesses of the wilderness. As to the aborigines' land claims, he says: "The aborigines don't own the land; the land owns them."

The natives in *Gods Must Be Crazy* are equally content. Only, the reality of apartheid is a lot uglier. As anthropologists Richard B. Lee and Toby Volkman point out, "The Bushman as Noble Savage is a peculiar piece of white South African racial mythology."[10] They demonstrate the contrasts between the fantasy !Kung San of the film and the way they really are in the 1980s. "There is . . . little to laugh about in Bushmanland: 1000 demoralized, formerly independent foragers crowd into a squalid, tubercular homeland, getting by on handouts of cornmeal and sugar, drinking Johnnie Walker or home brew, fighting with one another and joining the South African army."[11]

Such dissenting opinions have not been in the forefront of media coverage. The film has been a runaway success and had a long run in Toronto. And it is not just children who liked it. Some colleagues of mine in the English department of an Ontario university could not see an ounce of racism in it. The film was for them an example of pure comedy and a living symbol of their belief that art and politics have nothing to do with each other. They could not see why the noble savage living an innocent, nonmaterialistic, nonurban life was offensive to me. For them the film was an unabashed criticism of the complex, machine-dependent urban life.

The stated and unstated meanings I see as a Third World viewer are much closer to the ones pointed out by Lee and Volkman than to ones seen by my fellow teachers of literature. It is galling to me to be told that !Kung San are content in their habitat when they don't even have one.

But the fantasy of the white man does not stop at the noble savage bit. His guilt, very much like Cooper's, makes him portray the native as voluntarily rejecting such bounties of civilization as the Coca Cola bottle. Now what could be neater than that? The white man can enjoy his consumerism and standard of life without worrying about the native's poverty because not only he likes his poverty, but also he rejects material goods since they destroy his harmonious lifestyle. What could be a better salve for the white man's conscience?

Equally interesting for a Third World viewer are the clownish portrayal of Marxist revolutionaries, who are ineffective, stupid and barbaric. They destroy the otherwise paradisiacal countryside in their frantic and meaningless flight from the forces of law and order. A Third World viewer wonders whether these are wishful portrayals of Mozambicans, Angolans, Namibians and ANC guerrillas. And how convenient to use the native to destroy his own countrymen. The insurgents are captured with the help of the Bushman hero's devices. Meanwhile the two whites in the film pursue such high-minded things as scientific experiments on elephant dung, dissemination of education to the benighted natives and, finally, romance.

The film is an out-and-out insult to the aspirations of the Third World people as a whole and particularly to the African people struggling for justice. It is disconcerting for a non-white Canadian to find that this longest-running first-run movie in cities like New York and Toronto has won acclaim from the pundits, unlike popular films like *Rambo* and *Rocky IV*.

Although a non-white living in North America must face several types of blatant and not-so-blatant racism, it is the cultural racism of the subtle kind that hurts the most. *Gods Must Be Crazy*, *A Passage to India* and *Out of Africa* are supposedly "better" movies. They do not propagate racism openly. In fact they are so seductive as depictions of lost paradises that they tend to disarm an unwary viewer. After all, what can be more apolitical than a man and a woman falling in or out of love? To the Western audience saturated with this theme, the films may seem totally innocuous, no more than travel promotion for these countries. In fact, many people, including my gas-meter reader, have commented to me about the lush natural beauty of India and Kenya as depicted in *A Passage to India* and *Out of Africa*. The films obviously did nothing more for these people than to provoke a vague desire to visit these countries.

However, that is not how Third World viewers watched them. There were angry responses in India and Kenya. India banned *Gods Must Be Crazy* on grounds of racism. According to *The Toronto Star* of March 26, 1986, Kenyans considered *Out of Africa* to be "a demeaning racist movie." It is interesting to contrast these reactions to those of North American reviewers who, while acknowledging that *Out of Africa* paid no attention to the greediest land grab, spoliation and disinheritance, went on to speak about its "epic" reach, its "sensuous" and "sensual" qualities. Their attention was focused on the romantic couple in the lap of nature. These two elements, sexuality and the grand sweep of the landscape, were what stayed in their imagination.

But what does stick in the mind of a non-white viewer? Sam Kahiga, the Kenyan reviewer quoted in *The Toronto Star* was deeply offended by the "positive image" of Lord Delamare, a man who once killed two Africans by running them down when they failed to jump away from his car in time. Kahiga says, "Such are the characters *Out of Africa* honoured."

It is instructive for non-whites and concerned whites to read what Kenyan writer Ngugi wa Thiong'o had to say about Isak Dinesen's *Out of Africa* in his book *Detained*. As he shows, Dinesen used an extensive animal imagery to portray Africans. His most acute criticism of Dinesen pertains to her use of Africa as a background for her erotic fantasies.[12]

There is no space in these films for the experience of victimization perpetrated by colonialism. No effort is made to sort out the mess of history. The Third World viewer feels nothing but a profound alienation and degradation upon seeing such films. The non-white viewer can only react with anger when, after seeing the marginalization and caricature of African people throughout *Out of Africa*, he or she hears Karen Blixen's voice-over in Meryl Streep's fake Danish accent: "If I know a song of Africa, of the giraffe, and the African new moon lying on her back, of the ploughs in the fields and the sweaty faces of the coffee pickers, does Africa know a song of me? Would the air over the plain quiver with a colour that I had had on, or the children invent a game in which my name was, or the full moon throw a shadow over the gravel of the drive that was like me, or would the eagles of Ngong look out for me?"[13] This emotional self-indulgence is a masterful example of possessive individualism. Of course, Africans remember Dinesen, but not in the images of high romanticism as she would have wanted. Ngugi's ruthless criticism of her writings is a perfect antidote for the sick sentimentality of the film.

At the PEN Conference in New York last year, Salman Rushdie was accused by angry American writers of being "prescriptive" when he suggested that American novelists should also write about their country's imperialistic relationship with the developing countries.[14] Indeed, that is a question many of us have on our minds. How is it that the West keeps churning out works about attenuated sensibilities while disregarding the havoc caused by relations of imperialism in the less privileged parts of the world? And then, to add insult to injury, not only does it deny its complicity, it transforms our denuded, depredated earth into a colourful backdrop against which the drama of attenuated sensibilities can be played and replayed.

As long as such relationships prevail, a Third World viewer like myself can only feel what Aziz feels at the end of Forster's novel: "Aziz in an awful rage danced this way and that, not knowing what to do, and cried: 'Down with the English anyhow. That's certain. Clear out, you fellows, double quick, I say. We may hate one another, but we hate you most. If I don't make you go, Ahmed will, Karim will, if it's fifty or five hundred years, we shall get rid of you, yes, we shall drive every blasted Englishman into the sea, and then, . . . and then,' he concluded, half kissing him [Fielding], 'you and I shall be friends.' As the Mau sky and the earth say, in their hundred voices, 'No, not yet,' . . . 'No, not there'. "[15]

However honey-sweet the discourse of these films, it does not make us friends. Their fictional space is as unsuitable for friendship and understanding as Mau. They only lead to heartache and anguish and a long chain of misunderstandings.

6. Bears and Men in Birney's

"The Bear on the Delhi Road"

Birney's "The Bear on the Delhi Road"[1] once again brings home to me the difficulties of cross-cultural communication. What is so normal for us Indians that we do not even notice it strikes the tourist poet as "unreal," even when he is seeing it with his own eyes.

The poem is a sort of report card to the armchair traveller-reader at home in Canada and belongs to the "marvellous" genre that began with the "discovery" of the new world: reports of "fabulous" lands, strange flora and fauna and equally strange inhabitants.

As an "object of affection," as Birney's phrase describes those his travel poems represent, I am not philosophically opposed to my land and people being rendered "strange." (If I were being facetious, I would say that a bear should respond to the poem since it is really the bear that is the subject of the poem. The humans are subsidiary.) After all, some sort of communication does take place when a non-native observes the native's modus operandi and pronounces them "unreal." She, by that proclamation, has suggested to me, who had thus far been totally blind to the "unreality" of the thing, that my culture's normality can seem totally weird to someone from another culture.

For example, "The Bear on the Delhi Road" made me search my memory for Indian poets' attempts in this direction. Although I could not recall a single bear poem addressed to adults, I could remember quite a few Hindi poems I had read as a child about dancing bears and that are being read by Indian children today, including my own child. They went something like this:

Come on children
The bearwallah is here with his drum

And his dancing bear
Come, let's go see him dance
To the beat of the bearwallah's drum.

The dancing-bear theme is a perennial one in Indian children's books. The representations present a pleasant spectacle: eager children surrounding a happy-looking bear with its benevolent-looking dance master. The scene is made to look as normal as a TV ad about a Canadian cat eating its dinner in a crystal bowl. Or a Canadian dog calling the supermarket on the phone for its favourite dog food.

With that kind of a cultural background which treats the dancing bear as a normal, everyday event in a child's life, I obviously came to "The Bear on the Delhi Road" from a different angle than most Canadian readers who read it from the bear's point of view, albeit as interpreted by a Canadian home. George Woodcock's response, I think, is quite representative:

[T]he bear emerge[s] as a kind of animal Samson, a figure at once of pity and pride, and all thrown into relief not by any extravagance of language, but by the power of the poet to render the strangeness, in the terms of his own experience and his reader's experience, of what he is saying, and to use that strangeness to provoke a sense of universality.[2]

While, from my adult eyes, I can see that the bear is an unfortunate victim and should not have been yanked from "his" berry-patch, what I, alas, fail to respond to is the "strangeness" of the scene. Animals and humans do not live separate lives in India. Humans exploit the labour of cattle, horses, monkeys, bears, snakes and birds all over India. Birney must have seen from the windows of his car umpteen bullocks hitched to the ploughs in the fields, umpteen bullocks, buffaloes and horses pulling carts and wagons. Why didn't he find them "strange" or "brutalised"?[3]

Perhaps one can say that it is the difference between the productive labour and entertainment that attracted the poet's attention. But then, why don't we have Canadian poets writing about animals in the circus? Or animals in the African Lion Safari or Marine Land and Game Farm? After all we see these places advertising their friendly dolphins and bicycling peacocks and dancing elephants every day on the TV?

What I am saying is that the anthropomorphized bear on the Delhi Road is no more strange than the anthropomorphized cats or dogs or dolphins or elephants or whales in the West. And so when I find a poet calling a bear "unreal" or "tall as a myth," I cannot call up the right "universal" response. We must either love or pity all animals or not single out some for special poetic treatment.

Granted that the poem also represents humans and is understanding of their predicament. However, the fact remains that it is the bear who attracted the poet's attention first and the title of the poem suggests that the poem is chiefly about the bear and only incidentally about the humans. The poem gives the bear a subconscious mind and its dreams of "the shadows of deodars" provide the contrast to the "hot dust" of the "bald, alien plain." The men, however, are given no memories of wives or children or villages left thousands of miles away in their need to make a living. Their motions as trainers are presented as cruel, undignified and voiceless. They "leap," pull at the bear's ring and flick a stick at "his" eyes. Their humanity is further diminished by the poet's comparing them with locusts (which has led a critic to say that the men are a plague upon the bear). If these men are so emaciated as to have legs as thin as those of the locusts, recalling in my mind images of cartoon characters with stick legs, how do they afford to feed the bear? And how do they have the energy to jump around, teaching the bear to "prance"?

For the reality is that the ownership of any kind of property in India, and the bear is property here, indicates a modicum of prosperity. These men are not beggars—and, in fact, Indian poets have written a number of heart-rending poems about starving and emaciated beggars. These men are professional trainers and can be expected to make a living that would at least feed and clothe them properly. Details like "spindly as locusts" sound especially inappropriate as men and women of Kashmir are taller and of bigger build in comparison to several other ethnic groups in India. And so the "spare / men of Kashmir," clever as the pun is, does not sound right to me.

Another problematic element for me is the absence of the drum in the poem. The bear always dances to the accompaniment of a drum.

Without a drum, I wonder, how are these men teaching the bear? I might also mention that the bearwallahs usually "talk" to the bear during the performance.

My inability to get the "right" aesthetic response for this poem, thus, stems from my cultural otherness. The poem is written for those who find dancing bears on roads "unreal." Since I have grown up with "real" dancing bears as well as their representations in my kiddie books, I have a hard time thinking of the bear as a "myth." Thus, the third stanza, which informs the reader that the bear is not going to be killed but taught to dance, is irrelevant for me since I had surmised that much by the details in the first stanza.

But if I were to overlook this cultural baggage that stands in my way of receiving the poem as some kind of profound statement about the nature of human and animal victimage in the face of inexorable nature, as scores of Canadian readers have received it, I would still have problems with the premise of the poem as well as its tone and its word choice. For example, I don't like the fact that the reporting voice is so detached from what it describes. The way the poem is shaped—an observer, struck by what seems like cruelty towards an animal, asks the readers to forgive the humans for their conduct because they are doing it for the sake of making a living— makes it read like an apologia for these humans by someone who does not need to make his living that way. And written for others who don't need to either. The poem thus renders the whole scene "exotic" or "marvellous." Words and phrases like "unreal," "tall as a myth," "fabulous hills," could only have been used by a traveller. In fact, I found the word "exotic" used quite liberally by critics responding to this poem. I must say that that word turns me off completely. For it removes those "exoticised" into the realm of "myth" and fairy tale, thus denying the fact that they may be poor, hungry, disease-plagued, and coveting exactly the things that Westerners take to be the normal amenities of civilized life. It is ironic that the poet who wrote "Sinaloa," a poem that satirizes the exotica hunters, should himself have succumbed to creating that effect, perhaps unwittingly, in "The Bear on the Delhi Road."

Birney's other travel poems, I think, do not exoticize or distance in the same way. The white traveller observing a scene is very much a part of the total picture in them. His racial and economic superiority are noted and ironically commented on within the body of those poems. That, unfortunately, does not happen here, even though Birney has told us that that is what he was trying to convey: "[A]nd then in two hours the words came . . . with which to lay those three ghosts, which were I think also the ghosts of my own multitudinous guilt feelings, as a well-fed Western tourist in a world of unimaginable poverty and heat and dusty slaving."[4] I don't think the poem conveys those sentiments. Instead, by creating binary oppositions between "man" and nature and "man" and animal, it abandons the world of politics, i.e. First World traveller, Third World realities, for a seemingly profound "universal" statement about "myth" and "reality."

Although I have read many interpretations of the poem, and of those particular lines about the difficulty of freeing myth from reality, I fail to make a satisfactory sense of the poem. What is the connection between freeing "myth from reality" and rearing "this fellow up" except that neither of the tasks is "easy"? Is it that the poet is comparing his task as separator of myth from reality with the task of the trainers? For the conjunction "or" does not make it clear how the two tasks are connected or whether they are performed by the same people. If it is the trainers who are supposed to be freeing myth from reality, then it seems to me that the poem, in making these poor men training the bear for a living into myth-makers, diverts our attention away from the material realities of their life. Instead of making the reader think about their poverty or the ingenious way in which they snatch a living from a hostile environment, the poem asks us to think about the timeworn theme of Romantic poetry:

O Lady! we receive but what we give,
And in our life alone does Nature live.[5]

It is this theme that most Canadian critics comment on. But I am troubled by this diversion of the poem from the lived "reality" of two poor Third World men to yet another statement about the problem of knowing. Insofar as these men become a metaphor for carrying this "heavy" philosopical statement, they are being misused. The poem, it turns out, is not about them or about their material life, but about the human tendency to anthropomorphize every thing. That may be a worthy topic in itself, but a better vehicle could have been found for it in a scene from the Western world itself. How about a well-fed middle-class woman kissing her mani-cured and coiffured poodle? In fact, I and many other Indians, find such scenes as strange as Birney found the bear on the road.

Poems like "Bangkok Boy" or "Letter to a Cuzco Priest" do not use their subjects as metaphors. They are about the harsh lives of the subjects themselves. And they are rendered with a self-deprecating irony, an awareness of the narrator's own complicity and privilege, an awareness of the tenuousness of Third World human life unnec-essarily shortened by poverty and disease, an awareness of global injustice, elements which make many of Birney's travel poems so complex. "The Bear on the Delhi Road" lacks those ironies, perhaps because while Birney interacted with the subjects of the other poems face to face, the subjects of "The Bear on the Delhi Road" were observed fleetingly from a passing car. I find a failure of imagina-tion in it. The words seem inappropriate and empty of emotion. After all, what does "tall as a myth" really mean, or the description of the two men as "peaceful," especially when later on we are told that they are not "joyous"? Is it that we are supposed to read "peaceful" as "peaceloving"? And how come "the brilliant air" in the first stanza that evokes pleasant connotations has been replaced by "bald, alien plain" in the third and "hot dust" in the last when the venue of the dance remains the same? And the repetition of "tranced" in the last two stanzas, once to describe the bear and then the "tranced dancing" of all "men," i.e. humanity, again fails to make sense to me. We are all, human and beast, "tranced"? We are all "dancing" to the tune of some invisible trainer? I suppose if one agrees with such sentiments the poem will make sense. But since I find such statements too "easy," clever means of diverting us away from the real problems of life like war, racism, sexism, imperialism, inequality, I fail to respond.

There are a lot of Birney poems I like. There are some that I love. Poems like "For George Lamming," "Letter to a Cuzco Priest," "Bangkok Boy," and "Cartagena de Indias, 1962," are, for me, among the world's best modern poems. It is because they do not indulge in easy generalities, do not use their human subjects as metaphors, do not erase the profound differences in the circumstances of first and Third World people, do not "universalize" the experiences of the narrator—in fact they insist obsessively upon the differences of race and class—that those poems achieve their status, for me, as profoundly moving statements on life in the last decade of the twentieth century. "The Bear on the Delhi Road" lacks those qualities and therefore is disappointing to me. The observer, or as Birney calls it, "the untouchable tourist,"[6] is nowhere in sight in the canvas here and the scene the observer paints is not the right carrier, for me, for the meaning the poet wants to impose on it. The meanings in the poems I mentioned above emerge on their own, without the heavy-handed hammer of the poet, so obtrusive in "The Bear on the Delhi Road."

As Birney himself says, the meaning of a poem "varies according to the reader's basic language abilities and sensitivities, his acquaintance with other literature and with the background of the poem."[7] So, it may be that it is my reading of the children's poems in Hindi as well as my response to the "background" that leads me to respond differently from the other Canadian readers of this poem and from Birney himself who obviously saw a lot more in the sight of a dancing bear and two men on an Indian road than I can who grew up seeing dancing bears and dancing monkeys and saluting elephants and snakes swaying to the tune of the snake charmers' music, all performed for the sake of putting food in some humans' bellies.

7. On Reading Renu:

Text/Language/Culture/Translation

During the last decade, the translation of literary texts has finally begun to draw critical scrutiny. An activity that had been considered a labour of love and a matter of individual decisions mainly, is being examined intently now vis-a-vis its claims to authentic renditions and its intentions. Important questions are being raised about the nature of the relationship between the original and the translation, about the importance of cultural context as a signifier, and about the difficulty of translating class and region speech markers of one language into another.

The Summer 1988 issue of *Canadian Literature*, in fact, was devoted exclusively to translation and discussed many of the problems mentioned above in the context of Canada. More specifically, it examined how English translations of Québécois writings processed Québéc literature and culture for the consumption of Anglo-Canada. One of the more thought-provoking articles in the issue, and one which made me wonder about the Indian situation in this regard, looked at the English translations of Québécois texts as acts of cultural imperialism which depoliticize and decontextualize revolutionary writers, transforming them into "figure[s] of bland universality . . . normalized within the English Canadian scene."[1] The Québéc writers and critics, according to this paper, are concerned that "the foreign character of the text, the text as Other," be not erased in the process of translation. They would like to see translations that are "open to differences, open to varieties of meanings, open to both the original cultural referential system and the one in the process of being created."[2]

As someone who has been reading texts in translation for a very long time, and who has also raised the spectre of cultural imperialism through translation elsewhere,[3] I empathize with the fears of the Québécois. And I feel pleased that these questions about the intention, effect, and relationship between the translator and the translated are being raised by the suppliers of the originals.

When I started to read *The Third Vow and Other Stories*—Kathryn Hansen's translations of short stories by well-known Hindi writer Phanishwar Nath Renu—I was curious to see how Renu's distinctive idiom would sound in English. I could imagine the extreme difficulty, if not the impossibility, of rendering Renu's speech rhythms that gain their special effect from his ability to encode caste, class, and regional variations. In fact, I agree with Hansen's introductory remarks: "Renu left behind a body of fiction which in its very intimacy with the rural life of India seems to defy effective translation into English. . . . [His] successful overthrow of literary Hindi can barely be suggested through the medium of contemporary English."[4]

Is the task of translating Renu into English doomed from the start, then? As I read on, I wondered whether translating the speech of Renu's rural characters into contemporary English wasn't akin to standardizing, let us say, the Black American idiom of Zora Neale Hurston's *Their Eyes Were Watching God* or Alice Walker's *The Color Purple*. I tried to imagine whether these texts could survive the standardization. I am afraid, I cannot think of a grosser violation of their integrity.

I don't think that reading Renu in Hansen's translation can be deemed that kind of a violation. For one thing, hers is a labour of love. She *has* tried very hard, and this reviewer could certainly appreciate her hard work. Nevertheless, her Renu remained flat and, often, almost unintelligible.

I decided to read Hansen's translations for their own sake first. As I had not read Renu in a very long time, I did not have much of an advantage over a non-native speaker. During this initial reading, I felt that "The Messenger," "The Insult," "Old Story: New Chapter" and "Uprooting" retained my interest whereas such well known classics as "Queen of Red Betel," which should really be "The Queen of Hearts" and "The Third Vow" came across as rather boring and pointless. "Panchlight," "Smells of a Primeval Night," and "Raspriy" were also rather nondescript reading experiences.

I then went to the originals. While I had read some of them before and others I read for the first time now, they all provided me the complex aesthetic experience I have come to expect from Renu. Why, I asked myself, did I not enjoy the English translations as much in some cases and none at all in some others? Was it Hansen's fault or was a loss of meaning inevitable in translation?

The next stage was to compare the translated texts closely with the originals. It was at this point that I began to think about the distortions and transformations in the English versions and whether it would have been possible to render Renu's stylistic and narrative peculiarities in such a way that his "otherness" could remain visible.

I believe that it would be possible to achieve these objectives. However, it would only be possible if the translator were philosophically committed to conveying that "otherness." It is here that the problem of cultural imperialism crops up. For example, Hansen as translator has made many decisions which she does not explain. Nevertheless, many of these decisions are responsible for the lacklustre nature of the translations. I now intend to examine them one by one.

One of Hansen's major decisions is to do away with the cultural specificities. *Gauna*, for example, is an important ceremony in many parts of north India. It is generally performed one to three years after the marriage ceremony and until the *gauna* is performed, the bride stays home with her parents, the objective being a postponement of marital consummation till the child bride reaches maturity. The ceremony of *gauna* is an important narrative element in "The Queen of Red Betel," "The Third Vow," and "Uprooting." However, in all the three stories, Hansen has translated it as marriage. If the purpose of doing a translation is to provide the readers from another linguistic and cultural background with cultural understanding, then that purpose is defeated when the translator erases such differences.

There are many such erasures in Hansen's translation. *Navanna* is rendered as "the ceremony for the new crop." It may be literally correct but it is flat. I wonder how it would sound if one were to substitute the word "Christmas" with a phrase like "the ceremony for the birth of God." Equally jarring to my ears is "shop lady" for *Sahuain*, a word which means a woman of the trader caste and denotes subtle nuances of rank and power in the village hierarchy.

Of course, words like these are important cultural signifiers and need explanations. Translators are often afraid of providing too many footnotes or too long a glossary. I believe that if the translators are not going to act as cultural imperialists, it is imperative that they do that extra labour themselves and demand that their readers do likewise.

We may not know whether readers really desire a text which has suppressed culturally specific references in favour of a so-called "readable" English text until they are offered a choice. I, for one, do not agree with Phyllis Granoff, the translator of the UNESCO edition of Bibhutibhushan Bandyopadhyay's short stories, that "One requirement of the translations be that they stand on their own without the cumbersome addition of footnotes. This meant that where required I have added to the original a line or phrase to explain a cultural detail that might otherwise have remained obscure to a Western reader."[5] This, to me, is the naked face of cultural imperialism and it is too bad that it happens under the auspices of UNESCO. I believe that when readers turn to translations, they need a guide into the particular cultural universe of the social order being described in that text. They need an ethnographer as well as a literary critic.

One of the most satisfying translations I have ever read has an eighty-seven page introduction and footnotes on every page, explaining important cultural, literary, linguistic, historical and political references in the text. It is entitled *In the Mirror: Literature and Politics in Siam in the American Era* and is a collection of thirteen modern short stories by Thai writers. Thanks to the "cumbersome" footnotes provided by the translators, I felt I really had an immersion in Thai culture and grasped the way these writers interacted with their cultural and literary tradition. I fully agree with this text's translators who say that without the footnotes "too much would escape some . . . readers."[6]

D G Jones, writing in *Canadian Literature*'s special issue on translation, says something similar: "The meaning of a poem does not reside in the poem alone, but in its relation to other poems, other forms of language, the whole semiotic code in which the author lives. Its meaning is largely a matter of the way it confirms, nuances, or subverts that code."[7] This line of reasoning goes against the assertion that translated texts can "stand on their own."

Since Hansen has not stated her principles, I do not know if the erasures I have mentioned were brought about so that the texts could "stand on their own." However, unlike Granoff's text, Hansen's text does not explain away everything. She does provide a useful and substantial glossary at the back and, as she mentions in the "Introduction," many Hindi terms for "kinship titles" and "everyday items of food and clothing" have been retained (p. 9). Nonetheless, this retention is not uniform through the text. For example, while "The Queen of Red Betel" retains *Phua* for denoting kinship, Hansen uses "Auntie" for *Kaki* and *Mausi* elsewhere. There are many places in her text where villagers use "Auntie" for *Mausi* and "Pa" for *Bappa*, and to my Indian ears it sounds really corny.

One may object here that the Western reader won't know the difference. I think, however, it is culturally significant for the Western reader to know that "Auntie" is too undifferentiated to connote the complex kinship relationships of the Indian family and social life. For example, urban kids call their grownup acquaintances "Auntie" and "Uncle." Many Indians see this as a vulgar kind of Westernization. "Auntie" and "Uncle" in a Hindi text, then, come laden with ironies and that is one reason why I find them inappropriate here. Secondly, as Hansen claims that this particular edition is for an Indian audience, many more Indian terms could have been retained:

> For this edition, I have revised the entire body of stories, bearing in mind the differences between the original North American audience and the present Indian one. More Hindi terms have been retained in the text, for kinship titles and everyday items of clothing in particular, and some American slang expressions removed. (p. 9)

It worries me that the North American audience did not have the benefit of Hindi terms. It means to me that the North American versions committed several more erasures than this text which is supposedly for Indian audiences. If it is really so, then I wonder why Hansen had to translate *Lachmi* as "the goddess of the fields" (p. 99), or *hukka* as "water-pipe" (p. 114).

Now I move on to a different kind of erasure. This has to do with Renu's creation of class differences through the use of English words and phrases as an important signifier. The illiterate villagers distort them beyond recognition whereas the urban middle class sprinkle them as indicators of their higher status. Kathy Mezei's article in *Canadian Literature* suggests that Québécois writers also use English words as a narrative device and when this usage in the original is not indicated in the translation, a level of meaning is lost. When Hansen "translates" these English usages into standard English ("drama" for *dirama,* "part" for *pat* etc.), that interplay of rural and urban, literate and illiterate, haves and have-nots which Renu is so good at intimating is completely lost. It would have made a great deal of difference to retain these English usages and their variations in pronunciations through inverted commas or italicizations.

Since this mixture of English words and phrases is an important aspect of Renu's narrative technique, their "normalization" causes a rather important alteration. Too much is lost, I think. A couple of examples should suffice here. In "Uprooting," the Patna-returned Rambilas wears a *tee-sat,* i.e. a "t-shirt," to impress the rural money-lender. An urban Hindi reader, seeing that word, realizes that although illiterate and poor, Rambilas has acquired urban airs. When Hansen translates it as "polo shirt," those two levels of meaning—one emerging from the urban Hindi reader's superior knowledge of English and the other from the consciousness of the character himself—are lost.

Thus Renu uses the pronunciation and difficulty level of English words to accentuate class and caste differences. They signify upward mobility, intrusion of urban influences in the village, relationship between the ruler and the ruled, and subtle changes in the consciousness of the characters themselves. Renu's characters firmly situate themselves through their pronunciation and choice of vocabulary. Thus, while Hirman in "The Third Vow" and Rambilas in "Uprooting" indigenize their borrowings beyond recognition, the political leaders and journalists of Patna speak a Hindi which is liberally sprinkled with phrases like "vigilance committee," "coordination meeting," "militant workers" etc. In the original Hindi versions, these choices are important in the production of meaning and I believe, like the Québécois critics mentioned earlier, that the translation must not obliterate them.

In the same vein, I have problems when Hansen translates *biris* as "cigarettes" in "Old Story: New Chapter" (p. 108), and *gamcha* as "towel" in "Smells of a Primeval Night" (p. 133). The Hindi words are not only not equivalent to the English words here, but, in fact, as consumer products, *biris* and *gamcha* mark the user as belonging to the lower class. Thus, the substitution creates an important change in meaning. Since Hansen does retain *biri* in some of the stories, I wonder why it was not retained in this story.

Another important signifier in Renu are line-long quotations from popular Indian film songs. These film songs are instantly recognizable to most Indian readers—the reach of Hindi films being pan-Indian—and, therefore, they work as important allusions. For example, in "Old Story: New Chapter," while transcribing the cacophony of sounds on Patna streets, Renu, along with the political announcements, advertisements of popular remedies and the latest bill of films at the local movie theatre, gives us a line of a popular film song, obviously being broadcast on a loud speaker. On the one hand, while this cacophony is a very accurate description of the noisy Indian street scene, on the other, the juxtaposition of political announcements about flood-relief with a silly film song is extremely ironical. However, when I read the translation, "What should I do, Ram, I got an old man. . ." (p. 105), it made absolutely no sense to me. Either this popular film song from Raj Kapoor's *Sangam* should have been rendered in the original, or a footnote should have been provided. In the same story, the line "Oh, my countrymen! Shed a tear . . ." (p. 111) also did not make any sense to me whereas it is impossible to miss its import in the original since it is a famous song of Lata Mangeshker's, recorded soon after the Indo-Chinese war, and it is said to have brought tears to Pandit Nehru's eyes. Once again, the reader of the English version will completely miss these ironic juxtapositions so cleverly set up by Renu.

I will give one last example from this story vis-a-vis the importance of rendering cultural codes before I move on to other aspects of the translation. On page 111, Hansen has translated the Hindi word *sarvahara* as "bands of common folk." The word *sarvahara* literally means "one who has lost everything," and is used in India by Marxists and Socialists in the sense of "the dispossessed." Hansen's choice here, therefore, seriously dilutes the political force of Renu's story.

The details discussed thus far refer to Hansen's standardization of Renu's polysemic linguistic usage. Renu's four linguistic registers—literary Hindi, dialect, educated English and pidgin English—create various levels of ironic clashes, and when flattened into the "normalcy" of standard English, get completely erased. It should be possible to communicate these registers with the help of italicizations, inverted commas, and extensive footnotes.

Rendering Renu's stylistic features, however, would need less obvious tools, although they are equally important in terms of communicating the specific features of a Renu text. Here, too, I have problems with what Hansen has done. For example, a very important feature of Renu's style is the extensive use of sentence fragments, often ending in exclamation marks. It is a style reminiscent of D H Lawrence and evokes a sense of immediacy and excitement. This piling of sentence fragments is also responsible, to a great extent, for the lyricism of Renu's prose. When Hansen renders these sentence fragments into grammatically correct syntactical units, the result is monotony. To illustrate the difference in stylistic terms, I give below an extract from Hansen's translation in "Old Story: New Chapter," followed by my translation:

Along the banks of the Kari Kosi's tributaries—the Panar, Bakra, Lohandra and Mahanadi rivers—the fields of paddy, corn, and jute were a luscious deep green, as if painted by an artist's thick brush. Charming songs of the Madhushravani festival resounded among the mango groves and in the courtyards of the villages. The air was filled with the intoxicating fragrance of the finery of new brides—red, pink, and yellow saris drying and flapping in the breeze. (p. 98)

A brush stroke of deep green on the fields of September paddy, corn and jute along the banks of Panar, Bakra, Lohandra and Mahanadi—all tributaries of Kari Kosi! The reverberations of charming songs of the Madhushravani festival in the mango groves and courtyards of the village! The intoxicating fragrance in the air of the flapping and drying red, pink and yellow chunaris of new brides![8]

I think Hansen betrays Renu when she quietly converts his sentence fragments into full-blown sentences. Another equally serious betrayal is her consistent use of the past tense when Renu predominantly uses the present. This decision on Hansen's part has very unfortunate consequences in two ways: (1) it makes the English version sound like a recollection of a distant past rather than of the immediate present; and (2) it causes a certain awkwardness in the prose when it has to switch from past to present in order to render first person speech. Now, Renu's narrative voice makes remarkably frequent forays between indirect narration and direct speech of the characters. In Hansen's translation, first-person speeches often disappear. A comparison between the following renditions, first Hansen's and then mine, will clarify my point:

> Some said that Misar's eldest son was about to open a flour mill, and Rambilas was to be the manager.
> Some said that the householders in the village had gotten together and secretly bribed Rambilas. All the farmhands and herders were about to run off.
> Some said that Rambilas had gotten involved with a sweeper woman in Patna, and that was why he didn't want to go back. She was pregnant. (p. 130)

> [. . .] I've heard that Misar's eldest son is going to start a flour mill. Rambilas will be the manager.
> [. . .] I heard that the householders in the village have quietly bribed Rambilas. Because all the farmhands and herders were running away.
> [. . .] I hear that Rambilas had got involved with a "domin" and that's why he doesn't want to go back. The "domin" is pregnant.[9]

In this example from "Uprooting," Renu has given us the voices of several villagers. Renu's narrative discourse is obviously polyphonic and mimetic in the sense that he consistently prefers first person speech to indirect narration. When Hansen renders these first person speeches in indirect narration, she erases the polyphonous quality of Renu's narrative discourse.

The ellipses I have used in my translation are another distinctive feature of Renu's style. He rarely uses inverted commas to enclose first-person speech. Instead, the transition from indirect narration to first-person speech is marked through ellipses. They also serve the rhetorical function of summarizing. An ironic effect is created, for example, when the speeches of political leaders in "Old Story: New Chapter" are punctuated by a large number of ellipses, thereby making these speeches seem cliché-ridden and not worth reporting in full. Renu also uses them to effect transition from one memory to another in the interior monologues of the characters. The ellipses are, then, an important aspect of Renu's narrative technique and their absence in the English translation causes a considerable impoverishment of Renu's textual richness. It also causes problems in terms of intelligibility as there is no way of comprehending the transitions in time and subject matter without them.

Hansen's Renu, then, is a Renu transformed beyond recognition. The English version, to me, seems lifeless, humourless, and, as I said earlier, often unintelligible. Reading Renu in English makes me wonder about the losses other translations may have suffered in translation and of whose textual richness I have no knowledge of because I cannot read the originals and see for myself.

I want to say to the translators that we, the readers, need help when entering a text from a different linguistic and cultural area. We do not want standardized and normalized texts. We want texts that retain their "otherness" and "difference." We need extensive footnotes that will draw our attention to these signifiers of cultural meaning: linguistic registers, puns, allusions to literary, historical, political, and sociological discourses, social mores, and so on. I do not wish to single out Hansen, for she is not alone in her practice. As I have tried to point out in the body of this paper, what is at fault is the assumption on the part of the translators that footnotes should be kept to a minimum.

While reading Hansen's translation, I also wondered how much cultural knowledge the North American translators really have about the cultures whose texts they have taken upon themselves to translate. Hansen often misses the idiomatic expressions completely. One of the most glaring examples is her translation of *lal pan* as "red betel," which is, of course, meaningless. *Lal pan* actually is a playing card belonging to the suit of hearts. *Lal pan ki begum* therefore, means "the queen of hearts" and not "the queen of red betel." Hansen often makes these literal translations. Thus *karwa tel,* which should be translated as "mustard oil" if it is to make any sense in English, is translated as "bitter oil." *Chhoti Chachi* should be rendered either as it is or as the "Youngest Chachi," and not "Little Chachi," as Hansen has it. *Munh baye* means "[her] mouth wide open" and not "head turned to the left" (p.101). *Hath malna* is to "rue over a missed opportunity," and not "they were tempted by the possibilities" (p. 104). *Kam ban chuka tha* does not mean "work was done" (p. 101), but "to have one's wish fulfilled." Again, *Kam kaise chalega?* does not mean "How will I do my job?" (p. 130) but "How shall we manage?" In the very next line, *Itné logon ka kam kaisé chalta hai?* should not be translated as "How will all these people get jobs?" but "How do so many others manage?" There are several such mistranslations in the book and they often render Renu's meaning unintelligible. Some of them are very serious errors. One of the most dissatisfying translations in this regard is that of the title "The Queen of Hearts," and I wonder if the reader will really comprehend the story.

Overall, Renu in Hansen's translation loses much of his vitality and much of his point. I am afraid too much has escaped Hansen and I don't feel confident that the reader of this text will really know Renu's distinctive voice. I do concede that Renu is not easy to translate because of his polyphonic and polysemic narrative texture. However, I do not think that a translator, sensitive to these stylistic nuances of Renu, could not have done a more satisfying job.

Alas, there seem to be few translators who show that sensitivity. I have not come across many translations that treat the reader as sumptuously as the previously mentioned *In the Mirror.* If the act of translation is not to become another exercise in cultural imperialism, the translators must make sure that they highlight the "otherness" of the original. What is needed is explication, not erasure and assimilation.

PART TWO

MINORITY CANADIAN WRITING

8. Ironies of Colour in The Great White North: The Discursive Strategies of Some Hyphenated Canadians

My title, by juxtaposing the word "colour" with the phrase "the Great White North," an affectionate appellation used by Canadians to denote the long, wintry face of Canada, creates ironic speech about race. As any perceptive user of language can see, the title is really a tongue-in-cheek description of race relations in Canada. By appropriating a popularly used metaphor about Canadian weather and bending it to suit my own purposes, I have created a racial "difference," a racialized discourse. By establishment of intertextuality with several non-white Canadian writers who also use this popular metaphor similarly, I have created another level of irony which will only be evident to my listeners if they are familiar with the characteristics of non-white discourse in Canada, both literary and non-literary. And since irony is generally a denoter of dissonance, discord, disrespect and difference, the metaphors suggest that I am not speaking about the officially sanctioned version of difference which elides the issues related to race by speaking of "Caravans" and multiculturalism but about tensions and disaffections based on race.

The official definitions of Canada, whether they be by Northrop Frye or Margaret Atwood or by those in Ottawa, suggest that we have one national outlook and one cultural theme. They assume that although we Canadians do come in more than one colour, it does not really matter. This rhetoric of identification claims that we are all immigrants to this land and, therefore, all Canadian literature can be classified as immigrant literature, "a mourning of homes left and things lost."[1] A cosmic irony is claimed for both the Canadian psyche and Canadian literature, an irony which emerges from "man's" unsatisfactory relation with the universe.

This viewpoint, of course, suggests that the irony is directed outside the inclusionary community called the Canadian society. It also implies that the problem is at the level of "man" versus universe—something that cannot be helped—and not at the level of "man" versus "man."

For me, numerous ironies, therefore, emerge when I come across the discourse produced by non-white Canadians. For they, it seems, by highlighting the conflicts between Canadians of different colours, belie the claims of unity and homogeneity made by the custodians of Canadian culture. In their discourse, irony is racialized speech, emerging from the social, economic, historical and cultural differences and disjunctions between whites and non-whites. Their ironic speech is based on the ironies non-white Canadians experience in their real life as members of a society which has given them the appellation "visible minorities." While the official cultural and political discourse claims that the visible minorities and the invisible majority lead a harmonious life, the ironic speech created by the non-white Canadians belies that. The simultaneous denial and demarcation of difference by the invisible majority creates the possibilities of ironic manipulation, the ones exploited in this passage of Himani Bannerji's "Paki Go Home," from her collection *Doing Time*:

And a grenade explodes
in the sunless afternoon
and words run down
like frothy white spit
down her bent head
down the serene parting of her dark hair
as she stands too visible
from home to bus stop to home
raucous, hyena laughter,
"Paki, Go home!"[2]

It is the two words "too visible" that make the poem parodic, a critique of the subterfuges of Canada's official discourse. If only they had called us racial minorities, the non-white poet would not have been able to ridicule them.

I am trying to suggest that the ironies created by the non-white Canadians are based on ironies experienced by them. They create parodies of the dominant discourse to indicate that its tonalities of glory, or patriotism, or moral superiority rub them the wrong way. The ironic voices of non-white Canadians are, then, not directed to God or universe, but to white Canadians.

In discursive terms, it means that the ironic mode used by non-white Canadians is parodic and juxtapositional: it echoes and mocks the acts and words of dominant Canadians. For example, July 1, the erstwhile "Dominion Day" and present "Canada Day" has been called "Humiliation Day" by Chinese Canadians because to them the day is the anniversary of the infamous Chinese Immigration Act. By naming "Canada Day" "Humiliation Day," the Chinese Canadians desacralize the dominant discourse of patriotism. The native Canadians create a similar parodic dissonance when they rewrite the national anthem by changing "our home and native land" to "our stolen native land."

Such discursive strategies create ironies that are experienced in a race-specific way by non-white Canadians. They may, of course, be experienced by informed white Canadians as well, but the modes of experience will be race-specific for them as well. The Chinese Canadians who respond to the irony implied in "Humiliation Day" will do so as victims of an injustice while the sympathetically disposed white Canadians may respond with the guilt of the victimizer. The race-specific irony, then, insists on dividing Canadians into whites and non-whites, as opposed to dividing them according to their ethnicity. The major marker is colour, as opposed to ethno-cultural diversity. It is so because colour, at least from the perspective of non-white Canadians, is a codification of privilege. Therefore, colour, and colour-coding, become major carriers of ironies in the literature of non-white Canadians. The following passage from Krisantha Sri Bhaggiyadatta's poem called "Big Mac Attack!" from *The Only Minority Is the Bourgeoisie* is a good example of how colour becomes a carrier of ironic meanings in non-white writing:

The paper said
The paper said
An American man

This side of the mexican border
Shot 20 children and others
in a MacDonalds Restaurant

We knew immediately
he wasn't black
There was no large photo[3]

Another poem in the same collection points out another aspect of this representational racism:

in the last two months
all the black people on
television cop shows
have been criminals (n.p.)

In both cases irony arises from the fact that non-whites can read between the lines and foil the strategies of the dominant discourse. Thus, when we non-white Canadians watch beer commercials, we never fail to notice our absence there. The happy scene of conviviality, then, is interpreted by us as that of racist exclusion. It is in this context that all descriptions of a non-white physique, as in "black is beautiful," become ironic.

It is ironic to ponder on the fact that non-white writers are always identified on the back page of their books by their racial difference. "Dionne Brand is a Toronto Black Poet," we are told on the last page of her poetry collection *Winter Epigrams*. White Canadian artists, of course, do not need to be defined racially. Does it mean that the white writers are writing for everybody, regardless of race? If so, then it is interesting to speculate on why writing the body is so important for non-white writers.

This self-identification by race *is* an important piece of contextual knowledge for understanding the work of the non-white writers. For example, when Dionne Brand entitles her poems *Primitive Offensive*, and the poems happen to be about her journey back to her African ancestry, about slavery, about South Africa, about black heroes such as Frantz Fanon and Toussaint, one cannot but be struck by the multiple meanings of "primitive": especially its use by

Europeans to denote Africans as savage and uncivilized. The title, therefore, is colour-coded, and parodic.

Brand uses African chants, African symbolism, African referents in the poem. It is, however, divided into Cantos. In so far as she appropriates a Western European art form to do entirely different things with it, she creates a parodic text. However, the degree and level of appropriation imply more of a rejection than an allegiance. These Cantos differ greatly in form and content from the ones we are familiar with. There is not a single reference to European art forms. On the other hand, the Cantos *do* present the oppressive nature of the relationship between Europeans and Africans:

> but I stayed clear
> of Bordeaux and Nantes,
> no more trading me
> for wine and dry turtles,
> oh yes
> I could feel their breath
> on my neck,
> the lords of trade and plantations.
> not me
> not Bordeaux
> not Marseilles
> not for sugar
> not for indigo
> not for cotton.
> I went to Paris
> to where shortarsed Napoleon said,
> "get that nigger Toussaint,"
> Toussaint, who was too gentle,
> He should have met Dessalines,
> I went there to start a war
> for the wars we never started
> to burn the Code Noir
> on the Champs Elysees.[4]

This Canto is, like Ezra Pound's Cantos, about education, but a totally different kind of education. It mocks Europe's postures of cultural and moral superiority from a "primitive" perspective. And in so far as the European metropolis is a symbol of cultural sophistication for white Canadians, a cultural mecca where many of them have gone in their desire to drink from the fountain, Brand's "primitive offensive" mocks at the values of the Canadian cultural establishment as well.

Different interpretations of the world and different experiences of history are, then, at the heart of the ironies based on racial differences. What promotes awe and reverence in the Canadians of one colour, arouses ridicule and contempt in those of another. What seems appropriate and normal to one group, appears dark and sinister to the other. Feminists here may recall the new readings of fairy tales to bring out their misogynic content. The non-white writers, on the other hand, appropriate fairy tales to comment on the experience of racism. In *Obasan*, Joy Kogawa provides a racialized version of the classic fairy tale "Goldilocks and the Three Bears":

> In one of Stephen's books, there is a story of a child with long golden ringlets called Goldilocks who one day comes to a quaint house in the woods lived in by a family of bears. Clearly, we are that bear family in this strange house in the middle of the woods. I am Baby Bear, whose chair Goldilocks breaks, whose porridge Goldilock eats, whose bed Goldilocks sleeps in.[5]

In Kogawa's version, the fairy tale becomes a myth about the last five centuries of the history of imperialism. The incarceration of Naomi's family at Slocan can now be read as part of a larger story of racism. Kogawa's appropriative act is similar to the one whereby many Third World writers have turned traditional interpretations of *The Tempest* upside down and appropriated Caliban as the heroic figure. It is also similar to the appropriative act of native Canadians when they destroy the proprieties of the Hollywood westerns by cheering for the Indians.

The non-white writers' texts persistently draw our attention to these cultural representations of non-whites produced by the dominant culture. Maria Campbell in *Half-Breed* describes the movie about the Northwest Rebellion from her perspective as a Métis viewer:

The movie was a comedy and it was awful: the Half-breeds
were made to look like such fools that it left you wondering
how they ever organized a rebellion. Gabriel Dumont looked
filthy and gross. In one scene his suspenders broke and his
pants fell down, and he went galloping away on a scabby horse
in his long red underwear. Louis Riel was portrayed as a real
lunatic who believed he was god, and his followers were
"three stooges" types. Of course the NWMP and General Mid-
dleton did all the heroic things. Every one around us was
laughing hysterically, including Half-breeds, but Cheechum
walked out in disgust.[6]

Those who produced the movie and those who participated in the
proprieties of its form do not see or experience any irony. The irony
is experienced by those who bring a different perspective on history.
I, as a non-white reader, for example, wince under the non-ironic
"normalized" racism of such texts as Nellie McClung's *In Times Like
These*, Charlotte Perkins Gilman's *Herland* and Charlotte Bronte's
Jane Eyre. And the celebratory tone of some feminist critics vis-a-vis
these texts becomes ironic for me since I can't pay my allegiance to
it as a non-white woman. Similarly, I feel that my race-specific
experience has led me to experience several highly appreciated
works of Canadian literature rather differently from the mainstream
Canadian experience . It is these ironic experiences which impelled
me originally to bring out my book *Towards an Aesthetic of Opposition.*[7]
    It seems to me that ironies based on racial difference are always a
reactive response to the dominant, white society. In that sense, the
parodic forms created by the non-white writers are not "complicit"
with those of the past in the same way as the ones created by
postmodern art of Euro-America. Instead of "complicity,"[8] we see
ceremonial acts of rejection. Marlene Nourbese Philip's "Oliver
Twist," from her collection, *Thorns*, is a good example:

man we was black
an' we was proud
we had we independence
an' massa day done,

we goin' to wear dat uniform
perch dat hat
'pon we hot comb head
jus' like all dem school girls
roun' de empire
learning about odes to nightingales
forget hummingbirds,
a king that forgot
Harriet Tubman, Sojourner Truth
and burnt his cakes,
about princes shut in towers
not smelly holds of stinking ships
and pied piper to our blackest dreams
a bastard mother, from her weaned
on silent names of stranger lands.[9]

There is no complicity in the poem with the romantic ethos of
Keats's "Ode to a Nightingale." It is part of the imperial baggage
that the poet must reject along with "Hector and Lysander /and
such great names as these" (p. 5). Philip's use of children's rhymes
along with the island dialect are part of her ironic strategy of ridicule and rejection of an arrogant, imperial culture. Further, its juxtaposition with "smelly holds of stinking ships" makes one wonder
how an English poet could have delved in such exquisite romanti-
cisms when his society was profiting by trading in human cargo.

The use of African chants, children's game songs and nursery
rhymes, dialect, the evocation of place names associated with African, Caribbean and South Asian history, and the naming of non-
white heroes (especially ones like Angela Davis who happen to be
villains in the discourse of the dominant media), all these become
freighted with irony when we know that they are a strategic and
ideological rejection of Western European cultural forms. The non-
white writers in Canada have been deeply influenced by the writings and other art forms of the Caribbean, Africa, Latin America and
parts of Asia, and in their establishment of intertextuality with
artists like Derek Walcott, Martin Carter, Pablo Neruda, Nicholas
Guillen, J P Clarke and Bob Marley, they step outside the postmodern tradition of Euro-America.

This artistic alliance is itself fraught with ironies when we realize that the Canadian critical theory is entirely Eurocentric. Canada's geographic location is in the Americas, but we do not hear white Canadian literary theorists or artists quoting Derek Walcott or Frantz Fanon, C L R James or Aimé Cesaire. We have French imports like Derrida or Lacan or Foucault, but we seldom hear Achebe or Soyinka or Ngugi being quoted. And because the dominant cultural community's evaluative criteria are exclusionary of the cultural currents of most Third World societies, it cannot, therefore, perceive the ironies of those non-white Canadian artists who draw their inspiration from these currents.

Irony, thus, is a way of speaking that creates exclusionary communities. On the one hand, there is the exclusion practised by those in the cultural establishment, and, on the other, there is the creation of a community out of a sense of solidarity with victims of similar cultural and racial oppression. The non-whites in Canada share many similar experiences despite their diverse cultures and ethnicity. First, there is the history of their colonial oppression, regardless of whether they experienced it in the Caribbean or India or Pakistan or Sri Lanka. Secondly, there is the common experience of racism faced by them in Canada.

It is this community which may be considered the target audience of the non-white Canadian writers. It is they who share the writers' world view and experience and, hence, "get" their ironies. As I mentioned earlier, the relationship of a non-white author to her or his audience is an ironic one. Very often, in this discourse, the writer uses "we" to stand for a particular racial/ethnic group whereas "you" or "they" very often stands for a white person or persons. This marking out of difference, as I said earlier, is ironic because the writers belonging to the dominant community seem to speak to an undifferentiated audience, unless they address themselves to gender and/or class divisions. For example, Maria Campbell uses "we" to stand for the Métis and "your people" (p. 9) implies the white community. The relationship here is not that of an "author"-ity with its racially undifferentiated pupil listeners, but a more problematic one of a member of an oppressed group speaking to those belonging to the oppressors. Feminist critics have tried to appropriate these voices for the metanarrative of feminism. However, it remains problematic and unappropriated because "your people" creates a racial divide instead of a gender one.

Since the voice of the oppressed, "the wretched of the earth," has been a muted one throughout history, only allowed to speak within the constraining parameters set by the oppressors, one can only speculate how they would have spoken without these constraints. However, since that possibility has emerged only recently, the discourse of the oppressed is full of cautions, understatements, and silences. And because the relationship between the victim and the victimizer is so conflictual, the discourse addressed to the victimizer may range anywhere from persuasion to total condemnation.

Claire Harris's "Policeman Cleared in Jaywalking Case" in her *Fables From the Women's Quarters* is a long poem about a fifteen-year-old black girl who was arrested by the Calgary police and strip-searched for the crime of jaywalking. The poet begins the poem by quoting *Edmonton Journal's* headline (which forms the title of the poem) and pro-police reporting. Then she provides the items that the newspaper and the Alberta law enforcement appeal board neglected to consider. It is only then that she can speak of her rage and we understand it:

> Look you, child, I signify   three hundred years in swarm
>   around me
> this thing I must   this uneasy thing   myself the other
>   stripped
> down to skin and sex   to stand   to stand and say to stand
>   and say
> before you all   the child was black and female and therefore
>   mine
> listen   you walk the edge of this cliff with me at your peril
>   do not hope
> to set off safely to brush stray words off your face to flick an
>   idea off with
> thumb and forefinger   to have a coffee and go home
>   comfortably
> Recognize this edge   and this air carved with her silent
>   invisible cries
> Observe now this harsh world   full of white works   or so
>   you see us

and it is white   white washed male and dangerous even to
               you full of
white fire white heavens white words   and it swings in
               small circles
around you   so you see it   and here I stand black and
               female
bright black on the edge of this white world   and I will not
               blend in
nor will I fade into the midget shades   peopling your
               dream[10]

Harris's poem enacts the drama of race relations in full. First we see the hypocrisy of the media and the government bodies when it comes to providing equal treatment to black Canadians. Then we see Harris's interpretation of these discourses and their juxtaposition with her own where black signifies the physical body, the spirit, as well as the experience of victimage. White, on the other hand, refers to a patriarchal power structure, in the control of white males. There are ironies in the "whitewash" performed by the people in power and their inability to control the black poet's rage. However, I feel that white women readers will experience an ambiguity here. Are they completely spared the poet's rage against "white works" because they are women?

Frantz Fanon declared that "I have one right alone: That of demanding human behaviour from the other."[11] The ironies of non-white discourse emerge when this basic expectation is not met. Their discourse, therefore, is obsessively centred on exploring the racial difference, attacking the racism of Eurocentric discourse and forging a positive racial identity that is grounded in the memory of the historical struggle of the community. As long as the right of non-white people to get "human behaviour from the other" is not granted, as long as non-white skin is a caste marker, as long as Canadian society's image of the norm remains "white," the ironies of non-white Canadians will continue to parody the assumptions of "Canadian" culture, literature, and social order.

9. South Asian Poetry in Canada:

In Search of a Place

In their introduction to a special issue of *Canadian Ethnic Studies* devoted to the theme of "Ethnicity and Canadian Literature," the editors, commenting on the "predominantly Anglo-Gaelic or French character" of the official view of Canadian literature, ask:

> . . . where are the fictional remembrances of the Chinese, the Japanese, the Greeks, the Finns, the Ukrainians, to name only a few?[1]

The special issue brings to surface "ethnic" writers whose work has not been accepted into the mainstream.

Canadian Ethnic Studies is not unique in arguing for a view of Canadian literature that is different from the received one. Several recent publishing events suggest the development of a real awareness in the intellectual circles of the pluralistic nature of Canadian society. *Canadian Literature* brought out a special issue on Caribbean writers in Canada in the winter of 1982, and the *Journal of Canadian Studies* published an issue on multiculturalism in the spring of 1982. One hopes that intellectual acts such as these will result in a rewriting of Canadian literary and cultural history. One may even look forward some day to a longer rejoinder to E J Pratt's "Towards the Last Spike" than F R Scott's short poem reprimanding Pratt for overlooking the role of the Chinese workers in building the transcontinental railroad.

A notable addition to this multicultural Canadian literature is the work of writers of South Asian origins.[2] These writers deserve to be acknowledged on the strength of numbers alone. Indeed, the number of South Asian writers active on the Canadian literary scene is quite astounding given the fact that South Asians, who are relatively new to Canada, account for less than 1 percent of the country's population. A very encouraging sign of the vitality of South Asian writing in Canada is the publication of journals like the *Toronto South Asian Review* and *Rupture*, which provide a forum for creative and critical endeavours. Unfortunately, however, only Michael Ondaatje has been officially recognized, and the rest remain virtually unknown. One other writer, Bharati Mukherjee, gained some notoriety with her farewell-to-Canada article in *Saturday Night*.[3]

In this article I intend to comment on the work of South Asian poets in Canada. Apart from Ondaatje, who needs no introduction, Himani Bannerji, Krisantha Sri Bhaggiyadatta, Rienzi Crusz, Cyril Dabydeen, Lakshmi Gill, Reshard Gool, Arnold Itwaru, Surjeet Kalsey, Suniti Namjoshi, S Padmanab, Uma Parameswaran, and Asoka Weerasinghe have all had at least one collection of their poems published. Indeed, most of them have published more than one collection.

Although these poets admittedly come from different parts of the globe—for example, Guyana, India, the Philippines and Sri Lanka—a number of links tie them to one another. There is the ancestral link to the Indian subcontinent that gives common racial features to South Asians and makes them recognizable as a visible minority. Also, there are several cultural practices that South Asians continue to share, however distant their connection to the Indian subcontinent may be. Finally, there is the colonial experience that originally scattered South Asians to all parts of the world.

These historical linkages emerge as some identifiable patterns in the subject matter as well as the technique of South Asian poetry. The recurrence of these patterns in the work of South Asian poets, and their relative unimportance in the work of other Canadian poets, makes South Asian poetry highly interesting as a literary phenomenon both in terms of its new perspective on Canadian society as well as its rather unconventional relationship with the dominant literary tradition. The South Asian poet may be said to possess that double vision which comes only when one is alienated from the dominant group: the condition of writers as diverse as Henry James, Theodore Dreiser, Richard Wright and Salman Rushdie. This outsider is painfully aware of the contradictions that the cement of a homogeneous ideology carefully conceals from a full-fledged member of the dominant group. Consequently, South Asian poets write less about man's response to nature, the woes of age and death, the joys and pains of sexual love, and other such staples of poets through the ages, and more about racism, poverty, discrimination, colonial exploitation, imperialism and ideological domination. Although some South Asian poets do write on these perennial subjects, their strength as well as their preoccupations are accounted for, I believe, in terms of their otherness and visibility.[4]

The otherness of South Asian poets means that they have come to Canada, in Dabydeen's words, "mudbound in memory."[5] These poets, coming from countries that have only recently emerged from colonial domination and are plagued by poverty and political violence, continue to write about their places of origin. Unlike other immigrant poetry, however, South Asian poetry does not indulge in nostalgia or in what the editors of the aforementioned special issue of *Canadian Ethnic Studies* termed "ethnic genealogy."[6] Instead of a romanticization of the lost Eden—and one does come across some of that as well—South Asian poetry attempts to draw the attention of the Canadian reader to the misery of poverty:

> loving you,
> I think of twisted, leprous hands,
> rains laying waste the year's harvest
> people shooting each other off
> in war
> or by accident.

> You think I have wandered off
> into a private land of pleasure,
> leaving you lonely
> in your turbulence.

> But love,
> I will join you,
> my lust a trifle late perhaps,
> when I have rebuilt cities
> and caused children

to be born perfect
in a loving world,

as you lie thinking,
how long will he take.[7]

Here it is interesting to note that the South Asian poet does not
remain confined by national boundaries but seems to identify with
the entire Third World, reflecting the sense of solidarity the Third
World countries have come to share because of their history. Thus,
Himani Bannerji from India writes poems on Victor Jara and Sal-
vadore Allende, and Asoka Weerasinghe, a Sri Lankan poet, writes
about the misery of the war-torn Sahelia:

Life wrapped by naked skin
moves feebly south,
the salivary glands
parched by desiccation
and each mouth
open to gobble the hot air.
They pass neo-middens
of man, bird and mammal,
smoking under the hot sun
all scaled and bare,
where there are no flowers to bear
the lily-smell of death,
of an African "quality of life."[8]

It is apparent from the above examples that South Asian poetry
abounds in images of violence, suffering and death. In a society of
plenty where obesity happens to be a national problem, a preoccupation with malnourished and diseased forms may sound distant
and jarring. The South Asian poet, therefore, has to make sure that
his poetry is firmly bound to the Canadian context. To ensure this,
he often so structures his poems as to join the two realms of his
experience in a meaningful way. Some of the devices he uses are
letters home that talk about Canada to a person who is a stranger to
Canadian ways; physical and spiritual journeys that, apart from

articulating the poet's own experience as an immigrant, also bring
in references to the historical journeys of the past, such as those of
the *Komagata Maru* and the indentured labourers; contrasts of season—where Canadian winter often symbolizes the death of poetic
inspiration as well as the lack of friendliness on the part of the host
society; and dreams joining the poet's life at home with existence
here as seen in his psychic life. This poem by Arnold Itwaru, for
example, contrasts the two realms through the conjunctions which
only dreams provide:

> Half-formed, malformed, they are there in my sleep,
> they are there when I awake. Explosions of
> clocks and faces, of flesh and bone. I run
> from them but they erupt before me. I see
> them, but what are they? I've tried to forget
> them, to tell myself I'm okay, you're okay,
> we're all okay, I've tried to reason
> them out of existence. . . . .

> . . . behind the pages, the pictures, the
> streets, children eat adults, adults eat
> children, they all eat garbage, morsel to
> morsel, blood for blood, spectres, caricatures,
> skeletons, corpses, tumescent in endless
> oceans[9]

Whereas the dream structure of the poem allows the poet to bring
in experiences so radically alien to Canadian life, his mocking reference to the bestseller *I'm Okay, You're Okay* effectively contrasts the
two worlds. With remarkable economy, the title of the bestseller
underlines the poet's disappointment with the affluent West's attitude to the developing countries. The poem, while mocking the
narcissism of the individualistic philosophy propounded in the
book, shows that the problems it deals with are those of affluence.
Thus, in counterpointing itself against an ironic allusion, the poem
gains multiplicity of meaning and resonance.

A number of South Asian poets use this strategy of ironic con-

trast. This they bring to bear on the poem through an allusion to a
shibboleth of the dominant culture. The following poem by Bhaggiyadatta is a good example:

> we came
> in 747s
> to sink
> to the bottom
> of the upheld mosaic:
> to push mailcarts
> ("beaverbrook started this way you know")
>
> . . . .
>
> the natives say it's initiation
> they did it to the irish
> the italian the gay
> but we are better
> niggers
> we take shit with
> a smile
> and a colour tv.[10]

Bhaggiyadatta mocks the equalitarian pretensions of the mosaic
metaphor as well as the favourite myth of North American capital-
ism: that of the self-made man. This satirical sparring against the
powers that be stands in contrast to the thematic concerns of much
recent "mainstream" Canadian poetry whose mood remains largely
neoromantic. Unlike the self-enclosed, meditative poetic mode so
popular among modern Anglo-Canadian poets, the South Asian
poetic mode is one of ironic relationships. The outside world is
brought into the poem to provide resonances and contrasts, most of
them bitterly ironic. The poems repeatedly confront and challenge
social policy. Sometimes, as in Bannerji's "Terror," the note is extremely dark. This poem gives voice to the suppressed rage as well
as the terror that South Asian immigrants feel under the oppression
of hate messages on telephone, broken window panes, and physical
and verbal assaults. The irony in the poem is deepened by Bannerji's
use of symbols derived from history and contemporary reality.

The symbolism of King George's equestrian statue in Queen's

Park in Toronto arises from the fact that it was brought to Canada from India after the latter decided to discard all visual reminders of its colonial masters. For this South Asian poet, then, the statue is not merely a nice backdrop for a photograph but a painful reminder of her past and her differences with the Canadian society:

> I think of my daughter, I grow afraid, I see designs against her deep-set into their concrete structures or embossed into their Education Act. The blue of the sky, the gold of the sun, becomes an Aryan-eyed blonde and her spiked heels dig into my bowels.[11]

The "Aryan-eyed blonde" with "her spiked heels" becomes representative of contemporary Canadian society. The figure is based on an actual woman, a member of the Ku Klux Klan, who used to march on the Toronto streets most frequented by East Indians in the company of KKK men, taunting, threatening, and terrorizing the city's visible minorities.

Judging from the tone and the subject matter of South Asian poetry, it can be said that the South Asian consciousness is out of harmony with the accepted beliefs and practices of the host society. This sense of being out of step results at times in bitter anger, as in Bannerji and Bhaggiyadatta, and at other times in playful mockery, as in Rienzi Crusz's "The Sun-Man's Poetic Five Ways":

> Who, brown and strolling
> down a Toronto street,
> came up against these black vinyl jackets
> with mouths hurling their *paki paki* words like knives;
> froze, then quickly thawed to his notebook:
> "Color of offenders' eyes: hazel, blue, blue.
> Hair: All long, like Jesus, down the nape.
> Estimated educational background: TV's *Police Story*,
> starring Angie Dickinson.
> Home address: Paradise Blvd., Toronto.
> Possible motives: Kicks.
> So much poetry in the trajectory of crow sounds."[12]

Even though the poem shows a tremendous sense of restraint in the poet's refusal to let his hurt show, the purpose is identical to Bannerji's in "Terror." The question implied is, how can a society that prides itself in its democratic institutions allow the existence of such injustices? The perversion of the message of Jesus and the emergence of the new "heroes" referred to in the poem casually hint at the moral decay threatening this society.

Perhaps only the sufferer can tell where the shoe pinches. Thus, although the "mainstream" Canadian poetry does not treat racism as an important subject matter, it is one of the predominant concerns of South Asian poetry. This short poem of Lakshmi Gill is very suggestive in its hesitant tone and its reference to the persona's colour:

blue ice
(O my Canada)
can I call
you mine
foreign sad
brown that
I am[13]

Yet another aspect of the immigrant experience for the South Asian poet is that of being dislocated in terms of social and economic class. Even an immigrant from an affluent background might have to undergo the humiliation of becoming "lower class." As a result, immigrant writing in general is more class-conscious than the rest of Canadian poetry. To cite again from the editorial of *Canadian Ethnic Studies*: "By portraying the immigrant and ethnic experience, which has often been lived in a working-class milieu, 'ethnic' writers have provided a thematic perspective that has largely been missing at the centre of Canadian literature which, academic and elitist, has given little space to the drama of class struggle and its individual tragedies."[14] The South Asian poet, of necessity, writes about his treatment at the hands of landlords and immigration officials, racist graffiti in public washrooms and his experiences at the workplace:

FACE IT   THERE'S AN ILLEGAL
IMMIGRANT

HIDING IN YOUR HOUSE
HIDING IN YOU
TRYING TO GET OUT!

. . . .

TRYING TO GET IN
ON YOUR AFFLUENT FANTASIES
AND FIFTY-CENT FEARS

(BUSINESSMEN CUSTOMS OFFICIALS
DARK GLASSES INDUSTRIAL AVIATION
POLICEMEN ILLEGAL BACHELORETTES
SWEATSHOP KEEPERS INFORMATION CANADA
SAYS
"YOU CAN'T GET THEIR SMELL OFF THE WALLS"[15]

Sukhwant Hundal's "A Letter to a Friend" comments on the persona's life in Canada in the context of the mythical images of the Western world's prosperity that circulate in the developing societies:

You might have imagined me
sitting in a chair surrounded by machines,
touch-pushing switches with my fingers. . .

How can I tell you—when pulling
the four-by-twelve-by-twenty-two boards
how they drag my body
and sap its strength;
or when holding in my hand a broom
taller than myself
I spick and span the floor,
I am reminded of the good old college days
when we used to rebuke the janitor
for blowing dust while brooming the floor.

Ironically, instead of sending this letter, which lets his friend in India know "the truth," the persona writes another letter "full of colourful lies," which hides how his "self-esteem falls apart into

88

dust."[16]

The poem is a poignant comment on the fragility of the immigrant's psyche, battered as it is by individual and institutionalized racism. It is not only the oppressive external forces that the South Asian poet writes about, however. The poems of Uma Parameswaran give vent to another kind of fragmentation of the South Asian's sense of identity. Parameswaran writes about the conflicts present within the family itself. While this, again, is a subject common to immigrant poetry in general, the matter is further complicated for the South Asian poet by the fact that South Asian children are precluded by their skin colour from merging unobtrusively into the society at large. Written in the form of a child's monologue addressed to his mother, this poem by Parameswaran brings to light the self-hatred of a non-white child confronted by a society unwilling to respect his "differentness":

Ma, you think you could change my name
To Jim or David or something?
. . . .
When the snow comes, Ma
I'll get less brown won't I?
It would be nice to be white,
more like everyone else
you know?[17]

Though the subject is extremely painful, the irony is deliberately muted. The appeal to the Canadian reader to do something about the state of affairs is made very deviously. Nonetheless, the poem is highly effective in its understatement.

Much of South Asian Canadian poetry, like this poem, bears the character of a rhetorical appeal, even when it does not address the reader directly. Ranging through various levels of irony, it insists on confronting the reader with the contradictions between the society's preaching and practice. Its achievement can be defined, in Kenneth Burke's terms, as providing us with a "perspective by incongruity." A good writer, Burke says, provides new insights by "violating the 'proprieties' of the word in its previous linkages."[18] As must be clear from the examples quoted thus far, South Asian Canadian poetry is, above all, a violation of proprieties. In its constant insistence on questioning the rules of the game, as it were, it makes us aware of the ludicrousness of several solemn ceremonies. Take, for example, Suniti Namjoshi's "Poem Against Poets," which shrewdly exposes the shortcomings of Western patriarchal aesthetic norms:

> I fall upon the thorns of life
> > I weep, I bleed
> but to what Purpose?
> > There was once a poet
> who thought she was a nightingale,
> > and another
> who thought she was a rose—
> > charming perhaps,
> able certainly, having found at least
> > a way to cope.
> Would the nightingale's entrails
> > have been more powerful
> (as emblematic objects)
> > laid out on the floor
> of a room that you came to, and then
> > withdrew from,
> startled and amazed?
> > Oh the rose is bloodless,
> she is white with pain;
> > and Philomel wails
> in the woods again.
> > But there are the other
> more ordinary animals.
> > They are not literary.
> > They own their pain.[19]

The poem effectively points out the reasons many Third World writers feel so alienated from the Western literary traditions, even though they write in languages bequeathed to them by the colonial powers. Closer to home, it makes us aware of the structuralist-formalist stance of the literary criticism, so much in vogue in Canada, which dwells on images and symbols and other aspects of technique while disregarding the ideological and sociological aspects of literature. It also brings out the insularity of our departments of literature, which rarely tread outside the European literary tradition.

Himani Bannerji's "A Savage Aesthetic," a translation of a Bengali poem by Manabendra Bandopadhyay, makes a similar point. The poem is constructed in two parts. The first half of the poem is a lecture in a poetry class while the second half is the poet's rejoinder. The poem brings out the ideological stance of an aesthetic that prides itself in its objectivity:

> *"Remember, poetry too is architecture*
> *all else is redundant except the form, the style—*
> *what you call—the texture."*

> . . . .
> . . . and so the poetry class unending.
> Always the same. Sharp, academic
> an exhibition of smug narcissism. Full of apt
> and self-conscious quotations, allusions and message
> in a voice that plays with a joke or two
> calculating, avoiding emotional excess.
> So stands this hour of aesthetics, an exact reflection,
> of the confidence of the glass and concrete phallus
> that arises on an erased slum or broken shanty town.[20]

Such poems reflect the disillusionment of the South Asian poets with their Western literary training. For while their poetic strategies show their familiarity with it, their poems are really parodies of the dominant modes.

The South Asian poets invert Western myths for ironic purposes instead of using them seriously in the way Canadian mythopoeic poets like Jay MacPherson do, for instance. In "Lady Icarus," Dabydeen applies the myth to the story of Maria an aspiring immigrant from Equador who fell to her death when trying to escape from detention by immigration authorities.[21] Suniti Namjoshi's "Philomel" points out an aspect of the myth thus far unexplored:

> She had her tongue ripped out, and then she sang / down
> through the centuries. So that it seems only / fitting that the art
> she practices should be art for /art's sake, and never spelt out,
> no—never reduced / to its mere message—that would appal.

(Tereus raped Philomela and cut out her tongue in /order to silence her. She was then transformed into /the "poetic" nightingale that sings so sweetly through Western tradition.)[22]

The inversion of Western myths, the use of ironic forms, the retorts to Western writers and critics, all point out the South Asian poets' sense of the unsuitability of the Western literary tradition for their purposes. Itwaru, for example, clears out his territory by removing the familiar landmarks that the Western reader takes for granted:

NOTICE

ENTER THIS WILDERNESS AT YOUR OWN RISK. THERE ARE / NO VIRGILS HERE. BEATRICE AWAITS NOWHERE. THERE / ARE CANOEISTS, BUT YOU WILL FIND NO CHARON.
YOU / SHOULD BE WARNED THAT THE RIVERS ARE POISONOUS. / OTHER THAN YOU THERE ARE NO DANGEROUS ANIMALS.[23]

Itwaru, like so many modern Third World poets, professes that the idiom of Western poetry is insufficient as a medium for him. The long tradition that Western poets rely on in creating their meaning is discarded as so much jetsam. This has to be done because the tradition does not represent the history of a Third World poet like Itwaru. Of course, the poet discards it only symbolically. The things to be rejected have to be named if others are to understand this act of rebellion. Conventions have to be used if only in order to be stood on their head.

These constant inversions show how difficult the task of the South Asian poet actually is when compared with that of a writer who feels at home in his tradition. Salman Rushdie has described it in his novel *Shame* while expressing his frustration about rendering concepts of a culture in a foreign tongue that has no equivalents for them:

This word: "shame." No, I must write it in its original form, not in this peculiar language tainted by wrong concepts and the accumulated detritus of its owners' unrepented past, this Angrezi in which I am forced to write, and so for ever alter what is written. . . .

Sharam, that's the word. For which this paltry "shame" is a wholly inadequate translation. . . . A short word, but one containing encyclopaedias of nuance.[24]

Raja Rao, the celebrated Indian novelist, made the same point in 1937 while describing his efforts to tell a story from "the contemporary annals" of his village: "the telling has not been easy. One has to convey in a language that is not one's own the spirit that is one's own."[25] The titles of the works of South Asian poets indicate the nature of the difficulties they face in communicating their vision here in Canada; titles like *A Separate Sky*, *Distances*, *Shattered Songs*, and *Rupture* declare their sense of working against the current.

When the South Asian poet inverts accepted meanings, he is at least using a familiar idiom, though in a different key. But as one cannot remain in a state of perpetual reaction, the South Asian poet invents his own language. The difficulties of this task are well outlined in Dabydeen's "For the Sun Man," a poem addressed to a fellow South Asian poet, Rienzi Crusz. The poet commends Crusz for his ability to "pluck parables / from the Buddha's / core" while he himself, "being so much / like the West," is suffering from a loss of creativity. The poem states the need for creating new metaphors as the old ones no longer work.[26] The "Sun Man" the poem's title refers to is Crusz's mythic persona and occurs in several of his poems. The persona allows Crusz to amalgamate the two segments of his life in a meaningful way while it works as a readily available device with which to build further.

A number of poets "pluck parables" from their South Asian past. Surjeet Kalsey's "Siddhartha Does Penance Again"[27] compares the journey of a modern-day immigrant to that of the Buddha leaving home in his search for enlightenment. The poem plays with the difference between the two Siddharthas and the nature of their journeys. Suniti Namjoshi's *Feminist Fables* borrows its form from the ancient Indian tales of the *Pancatantra*. Using tales from the *Pancatantra* as well as from nursery rhymes, classical mythology, and the *Arabian Nights*, Namjoshi makes satirical comments on the place of women in modern society. It is a highly original work that is complex without becoming inaccessible.

Perhaps, for an uninitiated reader who has had no cross-cultural experience, the use of such resources will be difficult to comprehend. However, the South Asian poet is compelled to use them as nothing else can be substituted in their place. Uma Parameswaran's "Ganga Jal" demonstrates the importance of myth and ritual for poetry as well as the fact that language is not merely grammar and syntax but buried culture. For "Ganga jal" is a phrase that stirs some very profound emotions in a Hindu mind. It means the water of the holy river Ganga, which is needed in Hindu homes to perform several sacraments related to birth, initiation and death. Ganga water is poured into the mouth of a dying person, and after cremation the ashes of Hindus are strewn in the river. Every believing Hindu, hence, keeps at least a bottle of Ganga water at home. Given this context, the reader realizes by the end of the first stanza that the poem is about imminent death:

I heard him come in the door
And straight to the kitchen.
He had snowflakes in his hair
And his face was white as any neighbour's
All blood from it in his burning eyes
His boots formed an instant puddle
As he stood at the kitchen door.

Gangajal, he said, I need Gangajal.[28]

The poem captures a very intimate aspect of South Asian life in Canada. The household gods, the container of Ganga jal, the rituals of birth and death: who else will write about these aspects of South Asian experience except a South Asian poet? The poem is extremely moving as it dramatically renders the anguish of dying so far away from one's home and traditions. However, alien as its allusions are to Canadian readers, it is doubtful if it would have the same impact on a person unacquainted with the Indian ethos.

No doubt, a poetry that contains unfamiliar names of poets, gods, historical figures, Third World personalities, inversions of conventional poetic idiom, and, at times, rhythms and diction unfamiliar to the North American ear can seem obscure. However, if literature were taught in a multicultural context, as a means of promoting an understanding of the dependency of literature on culture, tradition, and history, South Asian poetry in Canada could serve as a useful means of comparison. It could then provide a valuable tool for teachers of literature in introducing their students to ways of apprehending the world that are different from the one they have been brought up with. Ioan Davies's remarks about the poetry of Bannerji and Itwaru can be applied to the contribution of the South Asian poets in general: "Their uniqueness is that they are representatives of a generation of writers in Canada who are not part of the mainstream of our literature." Their works, Davies goes on to say, are "the expressions of an otherness against a hegemony in which the terms of reference are dictated by the preoccupations of those who have established themselves as the centre-pieces of a dominating culture."[29] The act of making the dominating culture self-conscious is in itself a contribution that should allot South Asian poetry, along with the literature of other racial and ethnic minorities in Canada, an important niche in Canadian literature.

10. The Sri Lankan Poets in Canada:

An Alternative View

One of the most interesting cultural phenomena of the last few years is the emergence in Canada of the visible minority writer against the background of a predominantly "Anglo-Gaelic" literary scene. A large number of the so-called hyphenated Canadians are giving voice to the experiences of Canada's racial and ethnic minorities. These writers, coming from varied cultural and literary traditions, are not only challenging the erstwhile "official" cultural image of Canada, but, in the process of doing so, they are also introducing ways of apprehending that go beyond the Anglo-American tradition of literature that has dominated Canadian writing. Not all visible minority writers, of course, manage to be original and authentic. Many of them are lost to their communities when they find acceptance amidst the "official" bastions of culture. They, then, try to imitate the accepted ways of writing that will keep them in grants and on the poetry-reading circuit.

As someone deeply interested in the ideology of culture, I find it very fascinating to observe Canadian writers of visible minority backgrounds in terms of the processes of cultural domination. Their works, and their relative acceptance or rejection by the mainstream, are good object lessons in the politics of literary production. In their role of the "other," they compel us to take stock of Canadian literature from a vantage point that the mainstream Canadian critics rarely employ in their preoccupation with nuances of technique and their total disregard for such issues as history, politics, race, and class.

A study of the poets of Sri Lankan origin presently writing in Canada will bear out the truth of the remarks I have made. For, while as Sri Lankans they are being seen here as a group, a more motley group would be hard to conceive of. For example, Michael

Ondaatje is a name that would be hard to miss for a student of Canadian literature. But it is doubtful that this same student has heard of Rienzi Crusz, Krisantha Sri Bhaggiyadatta or Asoka Weerasinghe. These other Sri Lankan poets should also be of interest to the critic when analyzing Ondaatje's work, for comparison and contrast. This has not happened, since the mainstream Canadian critics as a rule disregard the categories I have mentioned above. Under the star system that operates in the area of Canadian criticism, Michael Ondaatje has won accolades for work of questionable merit while other Sri Lankan poets have not even received a mention.

In this paper, then, I have attempted to set a balance. I wish to assess Ondaatje's work in order to bring out certain disturbing questions that assail me when reading him as well as to comment, in some detail, on the work of his compatriots. As the questions I am going to raise have to do with some basic assumptions prevalent in the Western world about literature and its role as a social institution, my paper is also a critique of the predominant modes of criticism in Canada.

Ondaatje's work has failed to appeal to me. However, as a writer who has won several prestigious awards and whose work has inspired extravagant praise from established Canadian critics, his work continued to challenge me to pinpoint the reasons for my lack of appreciation. The result of that struggle was my paper (see Chapter 11), "Two Responses to Otherness: The Poetry of Michael Ondaatje and Cyril Dabydeen." Though the paper was read at the Learneds Conference at Vancouver in 1983 (and appeared in the *Journal of Commonwealth Literature*, Critical Issue, 1985), several more papers have been published on Ondaatje since then, reiterating the accepted view. Some colleagues of mine have taken my paper as a kind of joke and have teased me off and on about my stand on Ondaatje. I suppose joke is the only response left in the absence of a rational answer. Typically, when I asked one of them to describe what was so good about Ondaatje's work, all he could say was that this poet's line was so "cool"!

Such impressionistic appreciation does not really constitute an assessment of a writer's work. This, however, is the mode in which most critical commentaries on Ondaatje are written. Nothing is explained. Excellence is taken for granted rather than proved. As Sam Solecki is one of the important names in the Canadian literary establishment, and as he has written several papers on Ondaatje, let me quote a somewhat long excerpt from one of his articles in order to give the reader a flavour of this kind of literary criticism:

> He's among the handful of contemporary poets whom you can sense in almost any line of their work. In Canada, only Atwood has as strong a signature—an impress breathing in and through a line—colouring the work and establishing, constituting Camus' "climate." The climate of a world created book by book, never the same season, yet from *The Dainty Monsters* to *Running in the Family* always the same world.
>
> What changes is the creation of the illusion that his "exclusive" world is becoming less "exclusive," that the later work will "shave" the beard in the photo (*Coming Through Slaughter*, p. 133) and reveal a true "self-portrait." The illusion depends on one of the tricks he's learned to do; he uses valorized words like mother, father, sister, brother to distract the reader from noticing that for him, as for the best poets, "I" is a third-person pronoun, a word whose referents lie in the poem creating it for the occasion. Even *Billy the Kid* and *Coming Through Slaughter* tease the reader with the image of self as other, other as self.[1]

What I have gleaned from Solecki and other critics is that Ondaatje's poetry is concerned with the act of creation itself. The chief figure in his work is the artist who is seen "as gunman, as spider, as taxidermist, as Audubon, as cage-maker, as necrophiliac, as insurance executive, as collector, as editor, as suicide."[2] The artist, according to this point of view, is caught up in an endless dualism. He tries to capture "reality" and in that attempt "murders" it. The artistic process, then, is a series of disappointments and the artist constantly faces the danger of going mad. He lives on the "edge," doing a dangerous balancing act.

The trouble I have with this subject matter is that it is too limited to be made the basis of an entire *oeuvre*. Secondly, it is a rather romantic version of the artist who is always struggling against the onslaught of madness brought about by an "intolerable creative situation."[3] The artist in this version is not a participant in the social process, he does not get drawn into the act of living, which involves the need to deal with the burning issues of his time, such as poverty, injustice, exploitation, racism, sexism, etc., and he does not write about other human beings unless they happen to be artists—or members of his own family.

Ondaatje, the artist, makes poems out of other artists such as Victor Coleman, Wallace Stevens and Henri Rousseau. He writes about other artists who have become insane such as Buddy Bolden. He writes about historical figures such as Billy the Kid and Mrs Fraser, twisting them into exemplifications of his pet theory. It is amazing to see how one can write endlessly about the act of writing: what is known in fashionable circles as deconstruction. The poem is supposedly made and unmade in front of one's eyes. And it does not need the real world at all. Its subject is itself.

Coming from a cultural milieu in which literature is expected to say something about the world, I must admit that this kind of poetry fails to touch me in any significant way. While one or two poems on the act of writing are acceptable to me, to come across this as the "theme" in work after work is simply boring.

However, if inanity was the only problem with Ondaatje's work, it would not be so bad. What is particularly objectionable is his misuse of historical figures: figures whose lives have acquired a certain range of meanings and associations are appropriated by Ondaatje for a rather nonserious purpose.

The Man with Seven Toes,[4] for example, deals with the Australian legend of Mrs Fraser, a nineteenth-century white woman who was shipwrecked and spent some time with the aborigines in the bush before finding her way to the white settlement with the help of a runaway convict. Australian artists such as the painter Sidney Nolan and the novelist Patrick White have used the legend to comment on the injustice done towards the convicts and the aborigines by the Australian ruling class. However, in Ondaatje's version, such issues have been totally eliminated. Mrs Fraser is another one of those characters who have travelled to the "edge." The aborigines and the convicts are portrayed as rapists as well as uninhibited noble savages. The rapes, however, serve a positive role in the education of Mrs Fraser, according to Ondaatje and his critics. While colonization, which resulted in the oppression of the convicts and the extermination of the aborigines, has no place in Ondaatje's version, the poem tells us, in the words of Sam Solecki (if I use him so often, it is because he has written a total of five papers on Ondaatje, besides several sporadic comments and reviews), that civilization is very tenuous and chaos hides right under the veneer. Needless to say, such statements are presented as self-evident truths about human nature and civilization.

Coming Through Slaughter[5] purports to be about the life of Buddy Bolden, one of the pioneers of jazz. However, Bolden is interesting to Ondaatje only because he went mad and spent the last thirty years of his life in a mental asylum. According to Ondaatje, Bolden went mad because he never repeated himself, always trying to create his notes afresh. "Bolden's music was spontaneous, raw, impermanent."[6] Bolden, like the other characters of Ondaatje, lived on the "edge" because of the demands of his art. "He skillfully balanced order and chaos, creation and destruction."[7] In this Bolden, Ondaatje sees his own struggles with insanity and records them in a passage which is quoted by almost every critic writing on *Coming Through Slaughter*.

While detailed studies have been made of the imagery, texture, symbolism, allusions and whatnot in this work, no critic has asked whether Bolden went mad for the reason Ondaatje has given. Now I do not believe that writers have to give the literal truth. But as someone I met at the Vancouver Learneds Conference commented after hearing my paper on Ondaatje, Bolden's skin colour is entirely ignored in the book. *Coming Through Slaughter* makes nothing of the fact that Bolden was born only twelve years after the Civil War, or of the fact that jazz at this time had no appeal to the whites and that Bolden's audiences were entirely black. There is nothing in the book as to the fact that Bolden, though he was "King Bolden" to his black fans, did not exist for the newspapers or the custodians of the official culture. We do not learn from *Coming Through Slaughter* that Bolden wrote lyrics such as this:

I thought I heer'd Abe Lincoln shout,
Rebels close down them plantations and let all them niggers out.
I'm positively sure I heer'd Mr Lincoln shout.
I thought I heard Mr Lincoln say,

Rebels close them plantations and let all them niggers out.
You gonna lose this war, git on your knees and pray,
That's the words I heer'd Mr Lincoln say.[8]

One would not come across the fact in *Coming Through Slaughter*
that Bolden's mother had been a slave. The Buddy Bolden of Ondaatje has no colour. His problems are entirely related to his art. It
does not matter that he had become fatherless by seven and was
raised by a mother who worked as a domestic for white families. (If
one wants to know about the impact of such things on black artists
such as Bolden, one would have to read Billie Holiday's autobiogra-
phy, *Lady Sings the Blues*.)

Ondaatje has misrepresented black history and black experience
in the service of a very dubious cause. He has ignored three centuries of racism and oppression suffered by black people in America.
The distortions of *Coming Through Slaughter* become apparent when
it is compared with books by and about black musicians and seen in
the context of the heavy odds they struggled against. All this has
been ignored not only by Ondaatje but also by his critics.

Similar and equally dangerous distortions are present in *Billy the
Kid*.[9] Ondaatje does not explore the causes of Billy's violence. He
does not go into the nature of his relationship with the wealthy
Chisum family. He does not explore the Western as an integral part
of American culture. All we get here are close-ups of slaughtered
people. History, legend, culture, ideology are matters beyond Ondaatje's ken. And their misrepresentation has not been remarked
upon.

In *Running in the Family*,[10] the subject is Ondaatje's family, set
against the backdrop of his native Sri Lanka (which he refers to as
Ceylon). Elsewhere, I have criticized the book and its reviewers for
"exoticizing." I was quite pleased to come across a review by a Sri
Lankan critic who had similar reactions. Writing in *Kaduwa*, Qadri
Ismail, the editor of this University of Ceylon journal, says about the
book:

Orientalism, to simplify Edward Said's thesis, is the tendency
Western scholars have, when writing on the East and are unable to comprehend it fully, to go after the exotic element—in
the process painting a most inauthentic picture of what really

happens. This is not limited to Western writers however; Eastern writers—for many reasons—commercial and cultural, make the same lapses. Michael Ondaatje is most certainly guilty of this in his latest publication.

> This is the way most of the book is written. . . . People sent back from Oxford for setting fire to their room; men and women indulging—and how!—in fantastic drunken escapades; thalagoya eating and snakes running amok in the house; a mad and very drunk Major in the Ceylon Light Infantry running riot—and stark naked—in the Kadugannawa tunnel; the same man, drunk again, throttling five mongrel dogs; another woman, also drunk, breaking the necks of dozens of chickens. . . . They led most eventful lives, but Ondaatje doesn't bother to extract any meaning from it all. (Maybe it had none, but it is the author's responsibility to point this out.) . . . He calls Lakadasa Wikkramasinha a "powerful and angry poet"; in contrast, Ondaatje's poems which litter the book, are beautifully written—and insipid. He tells us nothing of the colonial experience—or of himself.[11]

Ismail's perceptive criticism brings out an aspect Western critics continue to ignore: would it not be worthwhile for them to find out what Sri Lankans might have to say about Ondaatje's work? For it, and critical responses to it, raise problems that writers and critics in the Third World have become acutely conscious of—the Western patronage of "exotic" writers and the resulting distortions in the local culture, the impact of Western forms in the colonial era and the Third World writers' need to break out of them, and, finally, the need to forge new critical yardsticks which confront the issues of colonialism and neocolonialism.

In her "Cultural Interaction in Modern Sri Lankan Poetry Written in English," Yasmine Gooneratne points to the pernicious effects of colonialism on the native culture. As in other colonized countries, "[t]he Sri Lankan reader of English was encouraged to ignore and ultimately to forget, the literary traditions of monastery, court and village that had accumulated over centuries among singers and writers of Sinhala and Tamil."[12] As a result, the "English verse of early twentieth century Sri Lanka is not only derivative and imitative of a whole range of European writers, but limited in its themes;

and these limitations stem from a crippling concept of genuine poetry as being the product of other cultures rather than of one's own, as well as from a severely restricted view of the function of literature as a whole."[13]

Gooneratne shows that Sri Lankan poets continue to face the problems of derivativeness and the colonial relationship with the metropolis. Ironically, Canadian literary values are such that these aspects are never taken into consideration.

When one turns to the other poets of Sri Lankan origin, one comes across a spectrum of attitudes and poetic strategies. One sees different levels of success in manipulating Western poetic forms to give expression to the identity of being a Sri Lankan and a visible minority in Canada. For these are themes untouched in the Anglo-American mainstream and the poet who wants to give voice to them must go elsewhere for tutelage.

Rienzi Crusz's work interests me because of the struggle that I perceive going on between his different voices. Some of his work *is* exotic and paints colourful portraits of Sri Lanka deeply swathed in nostalgia. For example: *see pg. 134*

When winter comes,
he crawls
into his sun-dial nerves
and sleeps
with myths and shibboleths,
as central heating steals
under his dark eyelids,

to dream of blue Ceylon,
where palms bend
their coconut breasts
to the morning sun,
and Nuwera-Eliya's valley
oozes with the fragrance of tea,
the sun-stroked fishermen swearing
under their salty breath
as they clown
with the rush of toddy

in their black skulls.[14]

Crusz has a good grasp of rhythm and word music, and knows how to evoke pleasing images; the passage is no more than a word picture. The winter-summer contrast is a bit too obvious and one gets tired of the sun-man formula. Then, like Ondaatje, Crusz seems to like writing poems about making poems, though not to the same extent. "Poem in the Light of Total Darkness" is a good example:

> Null and void are my drooping eyes,
> flamboyant hair, my gravel voice.
> Only the poem speaks
> with the sea's haunting boom,
> the delicate twitter of paddy-birds.
> Soon, the taste of honey and curd
> will grow in your mouth.[15]

"Poem in Peacock Blue," similarly, is about the poet musing on whether he will write his poem in peacock blue or red or yellow or aquamarine, etc.:

> Aquamarine, Tahitian,
> Robin's Egg, Delphinium Blue:
> sea colors cannot be trusted,
> they flirt too much, too fast
> with the moving sun,
> the magic fingers of the wind.[16]

Poems like this one are cloyingly rich in their imagery and euphony and short on meaning. I wish Crusz had more engaging themes to better utilize his technical virtuosity. For when Crusz does have an interesting theme, the results are extremely satisfying. At his best, Crusz blends his Sri Lankan and Canadian experiences to make profound comments on both societies. "Conversations with God About My Present Whereabouts" is an excellent poem, rich both technically and thematically:

> True, I often miss

the sensuous touch of fingers
on the shying touch-me-not,
the undergrowth's pink badge of bruise,
cacophony of crows,
the rain that pelted my thin bones.

But I am perfect now.
Seduced on shaven grass,
my barbecue glows
like a small hell,
the pork chops kindle,
the Molson cool,
I wear the turban of urban pride.[17]

The poem half humorously compares Sri Lanka and Canada as two ways of living. Crusz brings out the ambiguities of an immigrant's experience with great skill. The poem subtly criticizes the packaged, programmed life in a postindustrial society and implies that life in Sri Lanka, however hard in terms of material comforts, was more authentic.

"The Maker" is another poem which represents Crusz at his best. Multivalent in its ambiguities, it examines the meaning of colonial experience. It seems to ask: did the Maker create the black man of the colonized countries so that the white man could come and destroy him? In so doing, the poem makes fun of concepts such as "manifest destiny" and "the white man's burden."

Crusz's work, despite its uneven quality, retains one's interest because of the authenticity of his struggle to forge a voice that will be able to tell the world about a black man's life:

Dark I am,
and darkly do I sing
with mucus
in my throat.[18]

Asoka Weerasinghe is another poet from Sri Lanka who faces problems similar to Crusz's. Like Robert Burns, these two poets succeed most when they write about what is close to the bone, untrammelled by fetters of convention and propriety. However, while every poem of Crusz is polished and technically satisfying, Weerasinghe seems to write too much and revise too little. Many poems which begin very promisingly lose momentum by the final stanza, which comes as an anticlimax spoiling the whole effect. Sometimes the choice of a single wrong word destroys an otherwise worthwhile poem. One also comes across ungrammatical and syntactically awkward expressions which could have been easily corrected. But for these problems Weerasinghe could be a better poet. For he does write on a wide range of themes and manages to attain moments of beauty. One wishes he could sustain them longer.

"The Birth of Insurgents" is a good example of Weerasinghe's weaknesses:

> I was at home
> when April showered
> guns and bullets.
> Eight borrowed helicopters
> droned like ailing mosquitoes,
> while offspring of the guilty
> book-paddled in Paris and Oxford.[19]

The poem is ruined for me by "ailing mosquitoes." Its poignancy turns to bathos when one is forced to think about how to distinguish an ailing mosquito from a healthy one.

However, Weerasinghe, despite his shortcomings, has managed to write several good poems. His political poems are especially interesting. Poems such as "The Birth of Insurgents," "Looking Back," "Sahelia," "Drought" and "Mary March" read beautifully. "Dev (the child minstrel)," is quite representative of Weerasinghe at his best:

> An injured ivory-toothed serphina
> half his size,
> loaded on one side,
> strapped across the clavicle
> breathe into a voice
> the scrubbing hunger pains
> of a shrunken stomach.

The frail tawny arm
raised in humble salute,
he will sing en route
under a coconut palm
to a camel on burning sands,
for sweat-stained paisa
thrown from foreign hands.[20]

The poem appeals through its quiet simplicity which, nonetheless, is rife with ironies. Dev, the child, cannot assuage his hunger despite working hard at an early age, while tourists come searching for paradise in a country which cannot even provide for its children.

Poems such as "Dev" continue to attract me to Weerasinghe's poetry despite his lapses.

Krisantha Sri Bhaggiyadatta is a poet who has emerged relatively recently. His first collection, *Domestic Bliss*,[21] was published in 1981. Unlike Weerasinghe and Crusz, Bhaggiyadatta came to Canada when he was young (sixteen). His is a young and angry voice. Racism has been the most important experience in his life in Canada, forcing him to think about his identity as a non-white person from a country with a colonial past.

This thinking comes out in his poetry as biting satires on racism that all the rhetoric of multiculturalism fails to hide, on multinational corporations in their role as exploiters of the Third World, on the pious pronouncements of politicians that belie the practice of their governments, on the Western media that distort reality, and, finally, on those in his own community whom he sees as bootlickers of the establishment. Bhaggiyadatta's barbs and bitter ironic thrusts remind me of the poetry of the Augustans who attacked their rulers with great and savage gusto.

In poem after poem, Bhaggiyadatta manages to hold the reader with his gift of satire. His inventiveness is quite amazing. "What City? Ethnicity? Or How to Make an Ethnic Newspaper," for example, is over a hundred lines long and striking for the richness of its arsenal. Shaft after shaft comes raining down, each more powerful than the other. One recognizes in the poem a certain truth about politics in Ontario. In the effective portrayal of that truth lies Bhaggiyadatta's strength. The poem purports to offer a recipe for keeping an ethnic newspaper afloat:

Place as many photographs of the Prime Minister
The Minister of Immigration, The Secretary of State
For Multiculturalism, The Minister of Citizenship and
(then) Culture,
Federal Provincial Regional Municipal Leaders
The Parliamentary Opposition . . .
on the front pages

Scatter through the rest
Symbols of authority
Maple Leaves, Crowns, Crosses, Stars and Stripes . . .

Praise Public Relations Departments
from whom all advertising contracts flow
Accept ads on garbage-collection schedules
(for your dirty community)
Do not question terms of tender, supply and service
Lease and licensing, hiring and firing, taxes and
representation

Diversify instead

In group homes, nursing homes, homes for the aged
Blue and white movies, hair sprays/design/straighteners,
Cosmeticians, jewellers, spices, beauty salons,
Weight loss clinics, wholesale meat specials and bibles[22]

Bhaggiyadatta's poetry is markedly different not only from that of the other Sri Lankan poets who continue to use the Western lyrical-meditative mode, but also from the kind of poetry so prolifically being written in Canada: personal, slightly anguished, mournful about the past, laden with memories of childhood. As Charles Altieri commented in his *Enlarging the Temple: New Directions in American Poetry During the 1960s*, this lyrical-meditative poetry has narrowed down the range of poetic voices and divorced poetry from any active participation in the public life.[23] I agree with Altieri that modern poetry has been reduced to renderings of love, nature, metaphysics and imagination.

Of course, when one has a cause, or one feels deeply, one is angry. Feminists like Adrienne Rich have managed to break out of the mould. The black poets of America have broken away from the established forms to give voice to their history and their struggle. In Canada, minority poets like Bhaggiyadatta, Dionne Brand, Himani Bannerji and Cyril Dabydeen are engaged in something similar. When one reads their works, one comes across names from Africa, Asia and Latin America.

I specifically asked Bhaggiyadatta how he has made this journey when the dominant mode of poetry is so restrictive. He says he has been vastly influenced by black American poets who taught him to "curse." He says he is bored by the major names in Western poetry who have nothing to say about his life in the here and now, or how it came to be that way.

I find it very interesting to observe how a poet chooses his strategies. Bhaggiyadatta, for example, refuses to write what he calls "trees" poems. He says that though he is as affected by the beauty of nature as any other human being, he cannot separate it from his other experiences. Moreover, he fears that it is the "trees" poems which the anthologists and commentators will pick while turning a deaf ear to his political poetry. Bhaggiyadatta is a very promising and unusual poet. Though he may never crack the big league, he takes poetry to people who have rarely been spoken to by the modern Western poets. He recites his poetry at Toronto's Trojan Horse Cafe, union meetings, picket lines, the popular Kensington Market and informal gatherings. Poetry, he says, is one of his weapons in his fight for justice and dignity. Here is another example of his craft:

in the middle of the disappearances
in Argentina
when Canada was executing
a deal
on nuclear power,
the head of the

Atomic Energy Commission said:
the business of business
is business[24]

There are some other names that deserve mention. Tyrrell Mendis published his collection, *Broken Petals*,[25] in 1965 and continues to write sporadically. He is, however, a rather limited poet. His subject, according to the dust jacket of *Broken Petals*, is "love," "pain," "grief" and "frustration." He writes about what is known in the liberal parlance as "the human condition." This human condition, unfortunately, is too abstract and too melancholic. Mendis's new poems don't seem to be much different from his early work. He is a good case study in what literature curricula in India and Sri Lanka, heavy on the Romantics and the Victorians and short on the Moderns, do to our sensibility.

Siri Gunasinghe wrote some good poetry in the past. He is included in *An Anthology of Modern Writing from Sri Lanka* edited by Ranjini Obeyesekere and Chitra Fernando.[26] Poems like "Renunciation," "Dirty Dishwasher" and "The Water Buffalo" display a varied range and convey a feel for life in Sri Lanka. It is a pity, therefore, that Gunasinghe has stopped writing poetry. He has reportedly said that as a professor at the University of Victoria, he has become too comfortable. Unfortunately, immigration does choke creativity in many artists. We know about so many very talented writers, singers, musicians, painters and dancers who have given up, finding the transition between cultures and places too traumatic. Siri Gunasinghe's talent, then, has to be written off as a promise of the past.

Suwanda Sugunasiri, better known for his short fiction in Sinhala, has taken to writing poetry of late. His poems, published in the *Toronto South Asian Review*, show a remarkable control of the medium. He writes about his experience as a visible minority, about his fears and hopes for his children, and about events taking place in Sri Lanka. One hopes to read more poetry from him.

These poets from Sri Lanka are making a valuable contribution to the mosaic of Canadian culture. Their poetry, for all the strengths and weaknesses, is interesting and different. Their work, when put beside that of their "Canadian" contemporaries, raises questions that deserve to be seriously considered. These questions about ideology, about domination, about race and about class have been ignored for too long by the mainstream critics and academics.

11. The Poetry of Michael Ondaatje and Cyril Dabydeen: Two Responses to Otherness

A number of immigrant writers from the Third World are active on the Canadian literary scene. They have brought a refreshing diversity of subject-matter and style to a literary tradition that had been predominantly concerned with the two founding races of Canada. That homogeneity and consensus have been challenged by immigrant writers who often work as a disruptive force when they challenge the official image of a white Canada or when they direct their pen to issues such as discrimination, prejudice and racism.

While the number of Third World immigrant writers in Canada is impressively large, as I found when working on a bibliography of South Asian Canadian poets, not all of them get acknowledgement in terms of publication by a large house or critical attention from Canadian academics. Michael Ondaatje[1] is one of the very few South Asian poets to have been heard by the white audience. Not only have his works been published by better-known publishers, he has been the recipient of two Governor General's awards as well as critical acclaim in a number of articles by established Canadian critics. His poems are included in every undergraduate anthology.

This paper examines Ondaatje's work in the context of that by Cyril Dabydeen,[2] another Third World immigrant writer from a somewhat similar background. Both Ondaatje and Dabydeen come from former British colonies: the former from Sri Lanka and the latter from Guyana. Both of them have published several collections of poetry and prose. However, unlike Ondaatje's, Dabydeen's books have come out of small presses and remain basically unavailable in public or university libraries.

Though he has published in various Canadian journals and magazines and has given readings in Canada, and abroad, critical attention to Dabydeen's work has been nonexistent.

In examining Ondaatje's and Dabydeen's works together, I intend to probe the reasons for Ondaatje's success vis-a-vis the inability of Dabydeen and other Third World immigrant poets to be heard. It is proposed that Ondaatje's success has been won largely through a sacrifice of his regionality, his past, and most importantly, his experience of otherness in Canada—matters that are the stuff of Dabydeen's poetry. It is only recently, after a writing career of fifteen years, that Ondaatje has come out with an autobiographical account of Sri Lanka, but again, it is a book in which his relationship with his country of origin is highly problematic.

This absence of any reference in his major work to his past or to his otherness in terms of his racial and cultural heritage is very intriguing in so far as omissions in a writer's work are as meaningful as the givens. The significance of the omissions becomes clear when we examine their extent by comparing Ondaatje's work with that of the other Third World immigrant writers whose dominant theme is their displacement. The questions that must be asked are: how has Ondaatje managed to remain silent about his experience of displacement or otherness in Canada when it is generally known to be quite a traumatic experience? And, secondly, has this suppression affected his performance as a poet?

I have chosen to focus on Dabydeen's work in order, first, to assess the importance of the areas of experience omitted by Ondaatje, and second, to answer questions as to the aesthetic and political implications of the omissions.

In his review of Ondaatje's first book, *The Dainty Monsters*, Douglas Barbour gives us an interesting interpretation of Ondaatje's otherness:

> He owes much of his originality to his background, I think. The exotic imagery which crowds the pages of this book appears to stem from his childhood memories of Ceylon. His poems are jungle-lush. . . .[3]

The New Yorker reviewer of *Running in the Family* seems to have a somewhat similar impression of what constitutes Sri Lanka:

> It is a kind of travel book—eloquent, oblique, witty, full of light and feeling—that keeps spilling over into poetry, . . . into

fiction, into slapstick and high-class adventure. But it is only partly about the heat and mountains and jungle of Ceylon. Rather, it concentrates on the queer, wild, uncontrollable countries that Lalla and Mervyn turned their lives into.[4]

Just as India seems to evoke the image of the sacred cows wandering through the streets in the white man's mind, Sri Lanka seems to trigger the images of untamed nature.

The question, then, is whether Ondaatje's work contains more than "the heat and the mountains and jungle" of Sri Lanka that the white critics are unable to see in their ethnocentrism. For surely, Sri Lanka has more to it than the three things mentioned above. It consists of seven million human beings who ostensibly must have a culture and a world view unique to them.

Unfortunately enough, despite the publication of his recent book, *Running in the Family*, a book supposedly devoted to his search for roots, Ondaatje's work gives few indications of his Sri Lankan background. Ondaatje, coming from a Third World country with a colonial past, does not write about his otherness. Nor does he write about the otherness of the Canadian society for him. Intriguingly enough, there is no trauma of uprooting evident in his poetry, nor is there a need for redefinition in a new context—the subjects that preoccupy so many immigrant writers. One scours his poetry in vain for any cultural baggage he might have brought with him when he came to Canada. Also absent are memories of familiar places, people and things.

If one were looking for a cross-cultural experience, or a yardstick against which the "Canadian" writing could be measured in order to isolate the factors that make up its Canadianness, one would be equally disappointed. For here we do not see any bouncing off of one tradition against another, as we see in writers like Salman Rushdie. We do not have any references to writers of Sri Lanka or other Third World countries that would alert us to other ways of perceiving the world.

Instead, what we have is a poetry of the unmediated present. Ondaatje wants to catch hold of the passing moment without imposing any categories on it. The poem entitled "The gate in his head," ostensibly about Victor Coleman's poetry, gives us an indication of his poetic aims. The mind of the poet should try to approximate the immediacy of the felt response:

> My mind is pouring chaos
> in nets onto the page.
> A blind lover, don't know
> what I love till I write it out.
> And then from Gibson's your letter
> with a blurred photograph of a gull.
> Caught vision. The stunning bird
> an unclear stir.
>
> And that is all this writing should be then,
> The beautiful formed things caught at the wrong moment
> so they are shapeless, awkward
> moving to the clear.[5]

As in Wallace Stevens, a poet who appears in several of Ondaatje's poems, the reality is defined as chaotic and ever-shifting, a succession of random images and sensations. And the poet, whom Ondaatje defines as a spider, a fisherman, a murderer, is perpetually engaged in a Promethean attempt to trap this chaos without imposing fictional categories upon it.

Evidently, the poet in this version is so involved with the chaotic flux of reality that the past becomes irrelevant except for the pain it evokes in the poet for having passed away. Consequently, there is no history or memory; only a paranoid urge to catch hold of the passing moment. As a poem entitled "Billboards" tells us, the poet, or his persona, has a "virgin past" which is "disturb(ed)" and "invade(d)" by the present evidences of his wife's past:

> My mind a carefully empty diary
> till I hit the barrier reef
> that was my wife—
>
> . . .
>
> Here was I trying to live
> with a neutrality so great
> I'd have nothing to think of,
> just to sense
> and kill it in the mind.   (*RJ*, pp. 14-15)

The poem, supposedly funny, accurately describes the ahistorical nature of Ondaatje's poetry. His experience is not a collage where the past subtly intermingles with the present but eternally fresh. As another poem called "Walking to Bellrock" tells us, "and you swim fast your feet off the silt of history." Describing an experience in the wilderness, the poem emphasizes the pressure of the present sensations that wipe out the past:

> . . . there is no history or metaphor with us.
> The problem is the toughness of the Adidas shoe
> its three stripes gleaming like fish decoration.
> The story is Russell's arm waving out of the green of a field.[6]

This denial of history for the sensations of the present means that the poetic experience is always fragmented and antisocial. It cannot, consequently, carry the cargo of the poet's otherness. The past, of necessity, remains buried and unexploited, unable to give a sense of direction and coherence to the present which is continuously described as chaotic.

However, it is not just Ondaatje who suffers from amnesia. As Charles Altieri's *Enlarging the Temple* points out, the price of this freedom from history is "a loss of philosophical depth and resonance," and its symptoms can be seen, according to him, everywhere in postmodern poetry. The poets constantly in search of "numinous moments," of "the energies manifest in acts of intense perception," are unable to take in the social areas of experience:

> [M]orally an aesthetics of presence cannot suffice, however one manipulates it, because one needs abstract intellectual and imaginative structures by which to judge the present and to pose alternatives to it. . . . For no matter how acute one's sensibility, no matter how attentive one is to numinous energies, it is impossible to write public poetry or make poetry speak meaningfully about pressing social concerns without a return to some notion of cultural models preserving ethical ideals or images of best selves.[7]

Taking his models from Wallace Stevens and other contemporary

American and Canadian poets, Ondaatje is trapped by a style and way of thinking that perforce has to deny life in society because it is caught in a vicious cycle. The poet as "connoisseur of chaos" facing the "overwhelmingly anarchic or chaotic" "reality,"[8] then weaving his "nets" or "webs" to capture that reality, then realizing that the reality has slipped out or been distorted, is locked in a perpetual dualism beyond which his poetry cannot go. And since the exercise has been done to death, ever since Coleridge began it, it is beginning to get wearisome. As Frank Lentricchia puts it, this group of "connoisseurs of chaos" which includes such important modern writers as Wallace Stevens, W B Yeats, Robert Frost and such foremost critics as Frank Kermode, Paul de Man and Murray Kreiger, describes reality as "hostile," "violent," "black and utter chaos," and the poet as "an exemplary figure of courage and health" who confronts this chaos at the risk of self-destruction.[9] The posture, also adopted by Ondaatje and his critics, becomes quite comic for the reader when reiterated in such high sounding terms:

> . . . Ondaatje admires Bolden because the latter is an artist who has gone, for whatever reason, too far in his commitment to a demanding art. His sensibility was so compulsively responsive to the pressure of life's dynamism and confusion that in order to represent its complexities he took risks with his own sanity. In attempting to articulate aspects of this reality (both internal and external) Bolden went mad.[10]

To quote Lentricchia again, this heroic pose exudes "such self-congratulation about the plight of a modern, such arrogance, and such self-pity."[11]

However, one could probably put up with it, if a poet did not base his whole oeuvre around this apparently insoluble problem. Stevens and Ondaatje, unlike Yeats and Frost, do exactly that. Almost the whole of their writing is concerned with the idea of the artist facing the chaos. What Robert Lowell said of Stevens fits Ondaatje just as well: "His places are places visited on a vacation, his people are essences, and his passions are impressions. Many of his poems are written in a manner that is excessively playful, suave, careless and monotonous."[12] Of course, Ondaatje's critics find different words for the things Lowell is talking about. They call them irony, distance and control.

Both Stevens and Ondaatje demonstrate that art need not draw upon the outside world or the poet's own experiences. Thus, Stevens came to "write about arpeggios and pineapples rather than about racial tensions in Hartford or the practices of the insurance company he was vice-president of. . . ."[13] Similarly, Ondaatje, instead of writing about the reality of Canadian life or his Sri Lankan past, chooses to write about the "tension between mind and chaos" and the way it drives the artist to certain death. Even when he chooses specific historical figures, they become subservient to his dominant theme of mind versus chaotic reality. Billy the Kid, according to his critics, is the artist as murderer who distorts reality in his effort to capture it in static forms. Buddy Bolden, on the other hand, is the artist as victim who is destroyed by his single-minded devotion to spontaneity in artistic creation.

Here art has become truly self-reflexive. Poems are made about the act of writing poems. Or about other artists in the act of creation. Time and space, real lives of men and women, countries and cultures are irrelevant here. The question of otherness does not even arise as otherness can be experienced only when the self is in company. Once again, Lentricchia's remarks are very helpful to understand what is missing in this kind of poetry:

> The counsel of self-consciousness in the aestheticist mode does not urge the uncovering and bringing to bear of alternative perspectives which in dialectical interplay might offer constraints to the excesses and blindnesses of single-minded ideology. The counsel of aestheticized self-consciousness is, rather, paralysis and despair.
>
> . . . Somewhere along the line, however, we must ask ourselves whether this later version of aestheticism is sufficient protection against the claims—moral, social, political—that can be levied on the discourse of intellectuals, or, an easier question to answer, whether a tiny community of *literati*, cherishing the insulation afforded by their brand of self-consciousness has ever, can ever, or should ever want to make aestheticism operative in the world.
>
> . . . [T]he poetics of self-consciousness may not be much more, as Sartre suggests, than an apology for infantile behaviour

which must be judged accordingly because it is not being attributed to the legitimately irresponsible—that is, to the insane,
to the senile, to children.[14]

In other words, the metaphysical scarecrow of "chaos" has cut the
poet off from his fellow men in the ordinary walks of life. When the
poet sails "to that perfect edge / where there is no social fuel" (*RJ*, p.
70), and remains there, he is indulging in a self-willed isolation as
well as Romantic posturing. To judge this work as a heroic gesture
of defiance in the face of the universe, as Ondaatje's critics have
done, becomes a bit exasperating since when we place this discourse
in the company of other discourses, a sense of *déjà vu* is very hard to
avoid.

What I have attempted to say here is that Ondaatje's masters in
the art of poetry have led him away from an exploration of his own
realities. The Romanticist line of poetry is essentially ahistorical as it
sings only of the intensities of the present. These poets write in
universals: of Man and of what is called "the human condition" and
not of men and the conditions of men. That is, the poet does not see
the conflicts and contradictions dividing men but sings of man in
the abstract as though his life amounted to this one single act of
confrontation with what he calls chaos. There are no cultural and
historical determinants here. Man, wherever he may be, is the same
everywhere. Thus Ondaatje goes around the world to hunt for his
subjects. Billy the Kid, Buddy Bolden, Mrs Fraser and his father are
all "connoisseurs of chaos" and not situated human beings operat-
ing in a certain space and under certain historical conditions.

"Universal" is a highly approbatory term in the arsenal of the
Western critic. It performs the magic trick of eradicating whatever
may be troublesomely other. It creates a homogeneous world of
brotherhood, but at the critic's own terms. Whatever he suffers
from, he ascribes the same symptoms to us. The term, thus, is a
convenient shorthand for a person who does not want to come to
terms with the multiplicity and diversity of cultural modes as well
as differences of race and class.

Roland Barthes, commenting on a photographic exhibition called
The Family of Man, purportedly describing the unity of mankind
around the world through such universalist categories as love and
death, points out the hidden ideological stance in such laudatory

attempts at universal brotherhood. The analogy of the family hides what Barthes calls "injustices":

> Whether or not the child is born with ease or difficulty, whether or not his birth causes suffering to his mother, whether or not he is threatened by a high mortality rate, whether or not such a type of future is open to him: this is what your Exhibitions should be telling people, instead of an eternal lyricism of birth.[15]

The problems with the universalist poetic become evident if we examine Ondaatje's *the man with seven toes*. Here, all particularity has been sacrificed to make an archetype of Mrs Fraser, a middle-class white woman of the nineteenth century, the wife of the captain of a British ship bringing convicts to Australia. Her experience in the bush after the shipwreck becomes an exploration of "the borderline between form and formlessness, civilization and nature, the human and the natural and the conscious reasoning mind and the unconscious world of instinct."[16] "The poem," Solecki tells us elsewhere, "is the account of the confrontation with and gradual acceptance of the darker and more chaotic aspects of life which by the book's end are recognized as not only outside the self but within as well."[17] That is, we are asked to make of Mrs Fraser's life with the aborigines and the white convict a Jungian journey into the unconscious and forget about its political implications.

It seems to me highly unfair of both Ondaatje and Solecki that they trivialize Sidney Nolan's treatment of the theme, the Australian artist who inspired Ondaatje's work. While they use his name, as well the quotations from a book on him, they don't tell us that Nolan sees Mrs Fraser as a colonizer and presents the aborigines and the convict as victims of her class and not as Ondaatje paints them where they become rapists as well as embodiments of the irrational. Colin MacInnes's *Sidney Nolan*, the book that gave Ondaatje the idea for his own book, gives a highly political interpretation of the myth:

> This "betrayal" theme—in which the traitoress is portrayed naked in grotesque postures, and the stripes of her saviour's convict dress in skeletonic bars—is evidently one that preoccu-

pies the artist since he returned to it again in 1957. . . . And basically, perhaps, is an allegory of the conflict between the European expatriates who explored and governed and "squatted" on the land, and bullied and slew the prisoners and aborigines, but who never became the true Australians.[18]

In suppressing the political theme, in making Mrs Fraser a Jungian quester, in stereotyping the aborigines as the primitive and irrational, Ondaatje takes sides with the colonizer. He needs to realize that history, even when delivered "point blank,"[19] has a hidden ideological content which does not go away just by universalizing it. It is highly unfortunate that a poet originating in the Third World should be glamorizing the colonizers.

Raymond Williams in his *The Country and the City* shows how the Romantic landscape poetry turned a blind eye towards the people who worked in the landscape. Instead of showing the human beings in relations of production, what it shows is "a rural landscape emptied of rural labour and of labourers; a sylvan and watery prospect, with a hundred analogies in neopastoral painting and poetry, from which the facts of production have been banished: . . . inconvenient barns and mills cleared away out of sight . . . and this landscape seen from above, from the new elevated sites; the large windows, the terraces, the lawns; the cleared lines of vision; the expression of control and of command."[20] Ondaatje's *Running in the Family* is similarly elliptical. We are repeatedly given paradisiacal images of flower gardens, paddy fields, tea estates and forest reserves but no contemporary picture of Sri Lanka—which Ondaatje calls Ceylon—emerges. Williams's words on Trollope are equally applicable to Ondaatje's book: "What is seen is a social structure with pastoral trimmings. The agricultural poor are placed easily between the produce and the pleasures. And while this easy relationship holds, there is no moral problem of any consequence to disturb the smooth and recommending construction."[21] Reading *Running in the Family* one gets the impression that the other Sri Lankans—the fishermen, the tea-estate pickers, the paddy planters—are only there as a backdrop to the drama of the Ondaatje family which is described using the analogy of a Greek tragedy. We hear about the "race riots" because Ondaatje's uncle is directing an enquiry commission but we are not told what they are about. Ondaatje is similarly fuzzy about the student revolt in 1971 and its meaning. We are shown vignettes of people dancing in the moonlight to imported songs of the twenties. We hear about continuous traffic of people going to Oxford and Cambridge. We see Ondaatje's mother dancing in the style of Isadora Duncan, reading Tennyson's poetry and Shakespeare's plays. However, we hear about the independence only in parenthesis. We do not hear about the Ondaatje family's exploitative relationship to Sri Lanka. Their lifestyle is described in generalist terms like "everyone" or "people," which might give the impression to the unwary reader that everyone in Sri Lanka lived like that. Ondaatje mentions Leonard Woolf's novel about Sri Lanka but glosses over the sordid realities created by centuries of colonial exploitation as well as the inequities of plantation economy that Woolf's novel described so vividly.

Ondaatje's unwillingness or inability to place his family in a network of social relationships makes the book a collection of anecdotes which may or may not be funny depending on one's own place in the world. The reader who sees the Ondaatje family as belonging to the compradore class is put off by Ondaatje's sentimental tone and lack of perspective.

For me, the only redeeming feature of the book is the one stanza Ondaatje quotes from a poem by Lakdasa Wikkramsinha:

Don't talk to me about Matisse . . .
the European style of 1900, the tradition of the studio
where the nude woman reclines forever
on a sheet of blood

Talk to me instead of the culture generally —
how the murderers were sustained
by the beauty robbed of savages: to our remote
villages the painters came, and our white-washed
mud-huts were splattered with gunfire.

Ondaatje admits with a disarming candidness that this poetry represents "The voices I didn't know."[22] To me, Ondaatje's ignorance of these voices of otherness is a good indication of what is wrong with his poetry. Yeats said that one needed responsibility and allegiance to become a poet: "Poetry needs a God, a cause, or a country."[23] Lacking all three, Ondaatje's poetry speaks of ironies of perception in a voice that always remains calm and controlled. It is a poetry that has turned a blind eye to the realities of here and now in favour of a jaded metaphysics that is ultimately spurious. His case is a sad example of the cultural domination of Third World intellectuals who cannot see their world without applying imported categories to it. And he is certainly not alone.

If we contrast Ondaatje's work with that of Dabydeen's, we come to see the importance of the areas that Ondaatje has blocked out. Instead of locking himself into the Romantic no man's land, "the edge /where there is no social fuel," Dabydeen, learning from Robert Lowell, Wilson Harris and Martin Carter—the poets he says he has been influenced by—situates the individual experience in a community. He sings of the history of his community rather than of the naked individual in converse with the universe. As a member of an identifiable community, he sings of the contradictions and conflicts of men, men in power relationships, men as pitted against each other, as dominant or dominated by others.

Dabydeen's poetry shows that while otherness is alienating and burdensome, it also provides a unique insight because of the double vision the "other" can claim to possess. What seems natural and self-evident to the well-adjusted member of a society becomes highly problematic when seen from the eyes of an outsider. The outsider burrows under the suppressions of the dominant versions of history and myth and brings out their ambivalences and disjunctions. The other, thus, serves as a measuring rod against which a culture can take stock of itself. He serves as a mirror where a culture may see itself outlined as others see it. For cultural traits are inconspicuous to the members of a culture who remain oblivious to the dangers of ethnocentricism. If nothing else, the outsider can make a culture self-conscious and that in itself is a great achievement.

Dabydeen's "Señorita" is a good example of what an outsider's dispassionate glance can reveal. Having had the privilege of going to school in Canada myself, the poem touches a raw nerve in me:

This Señorita from the Dominican
Republic flashes a smile;

123

she tells me she has attended school
in Canada, is interested in Lope de Vega
and extols the Golden Age of Spain.

I remind her of Pablo Neruda
and Nicolas Guillen,
both closer to her home.
She still smiles, professes
a dim acquaintance with the poetry

of both, talks about water imagery
in Neruda. I remind her about the latter's
fire of love, the Cuban's revolutionary
zeal. She's not impressed.
She still smiles however.

How about the poets
of the Dominican Republic?
She smiles once more, "Ah, do you
not see I have been educated
in Canada?"she protests innocently.

"Five million people there—
surely there must be poets!"
I exclaim in silent rage.
Once more the Señorita smiles—
as bewitching as a metaphor.[24]

The poem's inclusiveness seems an astounding achievement to
me. Apart from attacking the apolitical and amoral stance of our
English departments, it also succeeds in showing, paradoxically
enough, the political repercussions of this apolitical stance in the
colonial situation. The formalist training the "Señorita" receives in
Canada has effectively cut her off from her native tradition. It prevents her from responding to the revolutionary message of
Neruda's poetry whose imagery she can discuss so glibly. No se-
verer attack could have been made on the Third World intellectuals
who so unashamedly live off the crumbs of Western learning while

remaining totally oblivious to their own heritage.

Ironically, Dabydeen's *This Planet Earth*, a collection full of poems as pungent as "Señorita," elicits a remark from the reviewer of *Canadian Literature* that echoes "Señorita" 's version of Canadian education:

> Though less versatile and sure in its treatment, it shares with *Divinations* recurrent dualisms, especially light/dark image patterns, a concern with the "ephemeral, trivial," with people who, monstrously closed in upon themselves, seek escape or transcendence.[25]

The truth of the poem's charge is self-evident. The critic has successfully neutralized the disturbing political context of the poems by using a universalist vocabulary full of abstractions and technicalities. He can only see "people" trapped in their self-made prisons whereas the poetry clearly assigns causes to their fate.

Another reviewer dismisses *Goatsong* because of its "obvious observations about poverty, love, and human cruelty."[26] It seems that until you become deliberately ambiguous and esoteric, the Canadian critic will not bother to take notice.

However, if Dabydeen's poetry seems obvious, it is because of the lessons he has learnt from Lowell who wanted to write poems "as open and single-surfaced as a paragraph."[27] The simplicity of such poetry has been won the hard way. The austerity and bareness of Dabydeen's poetry, its sparing diction and natural syntax conceal a craftsmanship which is amazingly effective in conveying his perceptions of the tensions and contradictions of the Canadian society.

"Lady Icarus," a poem the reviewer found trite and sentimental, is a good example of Dabydeen's method. Dabydeen dislodges a highly charged Western myth from its usual moorings to dislocate the reader. The myth becomes the carrier of a socio-political message for the first time:

> Lady Icarus
> "ordered deported—for the 5th time"

> You fell, you
> fell from seven

stories high
tempting gravity
from the Strathcona
hotel

not skyward
only landward

like a recalcitrant
angel, Maria,
all the way
          from Ecuador

you came, wanting
desperately to stay
in Canada

          so glorious
and free—defying
another deportation
order when suddenly
your rope

of sheets and blankets
broke
no sun now melting wax
your hold snaps

          as you plunge
to sudden death
we stand on guard for thee
oh so glorious and free

O Canada O Canada

                                        (G, p. 16)

     The myth and the national anthem provide an ironic structure to
the poem. The fact that Maria has escaped the immigration authorities five times in the past equates her determination quite effectively
with that of the protagonist of the myth. The phrase "so glorious
and free" could apply to both Maria and Canada because of the

syntax and makes the poem highly ambiguous in its accordance of a heroic status to Maria while being ironical about the anthem at the same time. The poem attacks the discrepancy between theory and practice and does it through a strikingly novel use of the Icarus myth. Further, though unlike Icarus, Maria is going downward when her rope breaks, her journey from Equador to Canada is truly upward. The poem hints at the mythic Canada that resides in the minds of many Third World would-be immigrants and a Canada, which, paradoxically, like the sun, eludes their grasp.

Instead of writing about the numinous moments of vision, Dabydeen persists in confronting the reader with facts of history which determine the direction of the present. However, the tone is not propagandistic and declamatory but intensely personal. Again, like Lowell, Dabydeen displays a knack of interjecting the intensely personal with the public and historic. "Fruit, of the earth," another favourite of mine, about a Guyanese family fallen on hard times, conveys a complex experience to the reader. While its lush imagery evokes the colours and tastes of the tropical fruit, the use of the past tense throughout the poem pulls against the images of plenty and speaks of a paradise already lost. The statement about the "balance of /payments" brings home the unjust deprivation the family has suffered. The poem successfully draws the contradictions of misery among plenty as well as subtly hinting at the problems faced by most Third World countries' economies. Also, the reader is forced to realize that the fruit this family has been deprived of, the title hinting a further irony through its Biblical echo, adorns the counters of our supermarkets. It seems miraculous to me that such a complex statement is made so cryptically.[28]

"Sir James Douglas: Father of British Columbia"[29] is a poem densely packed with the intersecting histories of Canada and Guyana and demonstrates the advantages an immigrant poet has through his access to two cultures. The poem is a meditation spurred by the poet's visit to Demerara, his birthplace, but which also happens to be Sir James Douglas's birthplace. The poem fuses the public and the private and the national and the global without any straining. It insists on pointing out the common colonial past of Guyana and Canada and the fact that they were ruled by the same family of rulers. The poem is also a good indication of the aptness of the title Dabydeen has chosen for the collection. *This Planet Earth* places Canada in a global framework, tied in a web of relationships and impinging on the lives and destinies of people of the Third World. The title, though it seems to echo McLuhan's global village image, actually subverts the happy pastoral vision evoked by that phrase. For the relationships Dabydeen is talking about are exploitative, the relationships of the metropolis to the hinterland.

Dabydeen's poetry can be called a poetry of subversion. It continually attacks the romantic, tourist-guide version of the tropics and uncovers the relationships of production. "Tourist Magazine" (*G*, p. 20), like Birney's "Sinaloa," contrasts the romance of the tourist paradise with the grim realities of hunger. "Ancestry" (*D*, p. 15), similarly, employs a nursery rhyme for ironic purposes:

The moon throws
light in the eyes
of half-naked children
A cow ambles along
and jumps over the moon
A sheep bleats in
blakean innocence
a song for master
and dame while
the little black boy
strides doggedly
along the caribbean
lane

The short stanza speaks volumes about the constraints of class on our perceptions. Dabydeen insists that we realize that the sheep's song, and wool, are for the master and the dame. By making the little boy "black," Dabydeen turns the nursery rhyme into a colonized's protest while the insertion of "caribbean" before "lane" firmly situates the poem.

The moon-drenched landscape reminds the reader of Dabydeen's ironic twists. It is used neither for Romantic meditations nor as a backdrop for the personal pains and joys. Instead, it becomes a means of drawing in the troubled history of his country. The ironic usage of the language of the masters gives it the satiric edge. Again, the poem pinpoints the meaning of the collection's overall title, *Distances*. The distances are racial, historical, economic as well as spatial.

Dabydeen's strong sense of history transforms everyday objects of our world into strangely disturbing symbols. "Molasses," for example, is a word that an ordinary reader associates with grandma's wholesome cooking. For the Guyanese poet, however, the word evokes painful memories of the colonial era:

> . . . I am astride a dolphinned ship,
> My muse gliding along, each hump-backed
> Wave carrying me farther away
> >   Middle passage again,
> I breathe sugar, molasses my skin
> The heat increasing in the Shangrila
> Of a new sun—
> A town's life burgeoning. Shapes and shacks
> I am the hovel of despair
> A crow flying low
> Circles the tenement life
> Far from Bombay.[30]

Dabydeen's poetry is full of references to sugarcane as well as other products of the plantation economy. The indentured labourers who were brought to work in the plantations recur frequently in Dabydeen's poetry as ancestral memories. The poem "Letter," describing the common immigrant experience of pain and unease when one does not hear from home, gains tremendously in depth and resonance by referring to the "indentured." The reference pulls in an entire chapter of colonial history which uprooted people from their homes so that the plantation owners could get cheap labour.

> You have not written
> these past weeks:
> a mail strike perhaps.
>
> I do not give up
> easily: remembering

old words

like salted cod
in the penury of taste.
And the dim slaves

with their leather
tongues; the indentured
also grew accustomed

to neglect
in the humid heat.   (*G*, p. 5)

Dabydeen's achievement, I believe, resides in making the condition of otherness accessible to the sympathetic outsider. In "Letter," for example, the grounding of the historical in the immigrant's immediate experience in Canada, and the fortunate choice of an image like "salted cod' which will also appeal to the Canadian sensibility make sure that the past suffering of the "dim slaves" will become real to a reader situated outside that history.

Another effective device is the use of names of historical personages and prominent Third World personalities. Jose Marti and Che Guevara rub shoulders with Amour de Cosmos and Sir Walter Raleigh. Their juxtaposition hints at the contradictions and conflicts that the colonizer's version of history overlooks. Again, the unsituated reader is lured by the names he might have come across in Canadian history books. However, the poetry shows us their unfamiliar side. Naming provides a resonance and complexity that works against the transparent texture of the poem. Though it is true that the unfamiliar names make the poems obscure at times, researching them is an added pleasure for a reader who wants to learn about the world.

The poem "New Life" (*TPE*, p. 64), referring to the poet's life in Canada, makes the statement that the poet's self is "mudbound in memory." This powerful image encapsulates for me the entirety of the immigrant experience in Canada: the past is not just the ethnic costume that one wears on ceremonial occasions but a visible badge that cannot be got rid of easily. More than that, the physical sensation of walking in mud-sodden shoes vividly captures the weight of the past the immigrant mind carries. The mud imagery also makes clear why Dabydeen's poetry sticks to the ground instead of taking off to the border realms.

The absence of the Romantic mode and its universalist rhetoric are thus deliberate. Like Lowell, Dabydeen seems to feel that "our world lies all before us and nowhere else."[31] A statement by Sartre is quite relevant to my point here. Metaphysics, he says, will remain "the privilege of an Aryan ruling class" for the time being as "one must be quite sure of one's rights in society to be able to concern oneself with the fate of man in the universe."[32]

The statement quite bluntly points out why the dominant mode of Western poetry remains metaphysical and why it has such limited usefulness for a poet so conscious of his alienation and his colonial situation as Dabydeen. His allegiance, as the collections amply prove, is with "those without power." He declares himself to be a "metaphysical socialist," a "humanist," concerned about "the improvement of man's lot in society," a position he ascribes to the fact of having grown up in a "semi-ghetto in Guyana." As a result, "the human condition" to him means "real suffering, real joy,"[33] and not just the existentialist nausea in the face of so-called "chaos."

The universalist vocabulary, in its rhetoric of identification and its blurring out of particularities, seems to me the crux of the matter. The universalist lives in an ahistorical, timeless world where the present simply repeats the cycle. For Ondaatje, whom I take to be a universalist, "theme," i.e. particularities of time and space, is "a minor part of the poem. If you read a love poem, well obviously there will be nothing new in a love poem—it's just the way it's said and it's the *way* it's said that makes it suddenly hit you."[34] However, as Barthes shows, it is the situation in which the love-making is carried out which is important as opposed to the blurring generality that love is part of a universalist human nature. There are people who make love on their pavement homes in Calcutta and then there are people who make love surrounded by candlelight and elegant furniture.

"The principal function of the universal in a colonial situation," Arnold Rampersad says, "is to destroy, defame, or defuse political analysis."[35] The poet who chooses to speak to all men, I feel, is only indulging in a fiction. He has simply refused to address himself to the particular needs of his community. The otherness is a fact of life and the universalist, by overriding it, is simply in retreat from the questions of ideology, power, race and class. It is only history which makes one confront these questions. And since history involves naming injustices, ancestors, acts of friendship and acts of enmity, it automatically calls for the poetry of otherness. Dabydeen's poetry is an encounter with history and hence with his otherness.

12. The Poetry of Rienzi Crusz:
Songs of an Immigrant

Rienzi Crusz, a Sri Lankan who came to Canada in 1965, had his first collection of poems, *Flesh and Thorn*, published in 1974.[1] The second collection, *Elephant and Ice*,[2] came out in 1980. In 1985 he published a third collection called *Singing Against the Wind*.[3] His poems have also been published in several national and international journals and he is the recepient of a number of awards.

It is often claimed that we are all immigrants to this land and that all Canadian literature is immigrant literature, "a mourning of homes left and things lost."[4] Such broad generalizations, however, fail to take into account cultural and racial differences among various immigrant groups, and the impact of these differences on creative expression. Nor do they differentiate between the literature of the second or third generation ethnic and that of the ethnic who has arrived on these shores very recently. And such differences are not insubstantial. The problems faced by "visible" ethnics are not simply those of a traumatic severing from their past as in the case of "invisible ethnics" who do not markedly stand out from the rest of the population.[5] Furthermore, the new arrival, unlike the native-born ethnic, is bound to be preoccupied with his own sense of identity rather than with exploring his "genealogy" or with "ancestor-seek[ing]."[6]

Rienzi Crusz's poetry is a good indication of how important these differences are. His poetry is an assertion of his difference. Like Yeats, he has created his own mythology and rhetoric because the available conventions of Anglo-Canadian poetry do not serve his needs. It is this act of self-creation that makes his poetry so interesting. Like so many other Third World Calibans who must perforce speak Prospero's tongue, Crusz wrestles with its inadequacies in order to communicate with the world from the vantage point of his

Atwood

otherness.

Crusz wears his otherness on his shoulder. There are frequent references to his skin colour in his poetry:

> Dark I am,
> and darkly do I sing
> with mucus
> in my throat
>
> (*EAI*, p, 90)

In another poem he speaks of his "black tongue" (*SAW*), an acute image of his separateness. Elsewhere he calls himself a "crow" (*EAI*, p. 53), a black bird whose frequent recurrence in Crusz reminds one of several West Indian poets.

This self-definition makes us feel that we are in a new territory here. The comfortable sense of tradition which a mainstream poet enjoys in his relationship with the readers from a similar cultural background, and which performs half of our labour for us—familiar allusions, a shared past, binding conventions—is unavailable here for it, being alien, will only falsify Crusz's meaning. We see Crusz doing a tightrope walk: speaking honestly in his unfamiliar "black tongue" but being careful at the same time so as not to lapse into complete obscurity or nostalgia, traps immigrant writers can so easily fall into. *that's not what you say in (y. 103*

Crusz never indulges in simple nostalgia for the life left behind, even though his poetry is full of beautiful evocations of Sri Lanka such as these:

> . . . blue Ceylon,
> where palms bend
> their coconut breasts
> to the morning sun,
> and Nuwera-Eliya's valley
> oozes with the fragrance of tea . . .
>
> (*EAI*, p. 36)

Though descriptions like these are an admirable indication of Crusz's technical dexterity, they are far more than word-painting. When placed in context, as parts in an overall structure, they also become symbolic. His Sri Lankan past becomes an element in a poem whose subject-matter is the poet's life in Canada. Most of his poems are built around a comparison-contrast structure so that the two halves of his experience are constantly interacting and modifying each other. The poem entitled "Conversations with God about My Whereabouts" is a good example of his strategy:

True, I have almost forgotten
the terraced symmetries
of the rice-paddy lands.
How the gods underfoot
churned in time
a golden bowl of rice.
A loss of aesthetics, perhaps.

But I am perfect now.
They have crushed the ears of corn
to feed my belly
white slice by slice
and all imperfections die
with One-A-Day and Vitamin B complex.

(*EAI*, p. 93)

The poem is built around these alternating stanzas in which Sri Lanka seems to symbolize a life lived close to the land amidst a plentiful nature while Canada stands for the bounties provided by the machine. However, Sri Lanka is not the perfect paradise despite its lush scenery:

I AM perfect now.

A brown laughing face
in the snow,
not the white skull
for the flies
in Ceylon's deadly sun.

(*EAI*, p. 95)

This sets up complex ironies, the implication being that the advanced capitalistic society which has removed all "imperfections" is somehow unreal in its evasions of the ultimate questions faced by human beings.

Poems like this are a good indication of the strategies an immigrant poet must adopt to successfully integrate the two modes of his existence. Perhaps no native-born Canadian poet has to constantly struggle with these dualities. Crusz's choice of titles itself indicates the magnitude of his struggle. The first two titles, namely *Flesh and Thorn* and *Elephant and Ice*, bring together two antithetical elements while *Singing Against the Wind*, emphasizes the isolation the poet feels in an environment that remains alien to his sensibility.

This sense of being an outsider, of not belonging to the charmed inner circle, results in a poetic stance that speaks in understatements and mild ironic thrusts rather than the impassioned hectoring which a Layton or an Atwood might feel no qualms about because of their positions of authority. I find it interesting here that Crusz rarely uses the pronoun "we" in its inclusive sense, a rhetorical device which allows the user to speak for the entire society. This diffidence, it would seem, is a characteristic response of the writers coming from minority groups. Myrna Kostash, a Ukrainian-Canadian writer speaking in a panel on "Hyphenated Canadians: The Question of Consciousness" at the conference on "Ethnicity and the Writer in Canada" defines it well:

> A negative feature of my book that some people picked up was the defensiveness of tone and a tendency to overstate my case. I can see how that could be interpreted as an ethnic characteristic, a sort of ghetto reaction, but it could also just as easily apply to the fact that I'm a Canadian vis a vis the American empire. . . . Similarly, is the defensiveness I show in writing about Two Hills a female characteristic . . . ? I am a female voice in a wilderness of masculine supremacy, so in the end, I don't know. But this generalized condition of somehow being an outsider, of being a down and outer, does come through.[7]

This difference between the tonalities of the outsider and the insider in any particular society is an intriguing one and literary critics need to become more aware of the consequence it has in the overall pattern of a work. The outsider, as Myrna Kostash points out, can never be sure of the right tone to adopt. If she is defensive and tending towards overstatement, Crusz's reaction is just the opposite. Unlike several other South Asian poets who might at times appear to be almost hysterical, Crusz constantly hedges behind understatements, even when a scream might seem to be a more natural response. And instead of making any direct observations on the host society, he structures his poems as journeys of the self: the self as it undergoes various transformations in the new environment, becomes a means of judging unobtrusively. Another related aspect of his approach is that the poems, instead of communicating with the reader on some topic of mutual interest, make statements about how difficult communication is, given the differences between the readers and the poet:

> It would have been somewhat different
> in green Sri Lanka, where I touched
> the sun's fire daily
> with my warm finger tips.
>
> I wouldn't have hesitated
> to call you a bastard
> and for emphasis, might have even
> thrown in the four-letter word.
>
>   (*SAW*, "in the idiom of the sun")

The efforts at softening a rather unpalatable message are very characteristic of Crusz. Even on the question of racism, a very important theme for several South Asian writers in Canada, and a theme which provokes extreme poetic anger from many, Crusz's response is couched in understatements. This is how the poet describes his encounter with racial hatred in a Toronto cafe:

> and meeting civilization head on
> with a doughnut, hot coffee, a cigarette.
> At the centre table,
> suddenly thinking of horseshoes.
> What if somebody mistakes me
> for a target
> begins to practise his Western art?

Cigarette smoke snakes above my head,
makes a highway,
collapses.

I'm being watched.
Blue eyes suddenly a torment,
a torrent of waterfall,
beauty with a knife between its teeth.
So once again,
I must close my black eyes,
feel my legs
climbing
towards the sun.
Each crag, jutting root,
now a rung of mercy.

I must move, move
away from this darkness unasked for,
or make that second discovery
of fire: love
for the tall man with thrusting blue eyes
seeing nothing
but a blur of shadowed skin
a spot on his morning sun.[8]

The poem is a remarkable achievement. Crusz has managed to articulate the subtler kinds of racist negations that non-white Canadians undergo on a daily basis. The poetic act of containment also suggests the price which the brown-skinned immigrant pays for maintaining a dignified front. The feelings of hate and anger must somehow be transmuted into laughter if one wants to function in the day-to-day world:

When hate wears
a white mud mask,
and dances in rituals
of living death,
he holds out a golden hand
marinated in the sun,

a Jesus heart plucked
from some ancient Calvary.

(*EAI*, p. 35)

I find it interesting here that Crusz, instead of directly accusing
the host society, personifies hate, thereby sublimating his anger, a
posture which other South Asian poets reject in favour of spilling
out their outrage. Both responses, of course, are resorted to by the
visible minorities.

Congruent with his response to racism is Crusz's response to
colonialism, another important theme in the work of South Asian
poets. Some South Asian poets lash out at what they consider to be
the complacency and the insularity of Canadians in this regard.
They write poems on historical events as well as present political
turmoil in the Third World. Crusz, characteristically, understates
the theme. For example, the poem entitled "Roots" which is ostensibly about the poet's mixed parentage, becomes a vehicle for an
oblique comment on Sri Lanka's colonial past:

A Portuguese captain holds
the soft brown hand of my Sinhala mother.
It's the year 1515 AD,
When two civilizations kissed and merged,
And I, burgher of that hot embrace,
write a poem of history
as if it were only the romance
of a lonely soldier on a crowded beach
in Southern Ceylon.

(*SAW*, "Roots")

The "as if," of course, opens a flood gate and the 450 years of
colonial history invade the poem. Nonetheless, the statement is so
muted that an unwary reader could miss it quite easily. The reference to ivory in a poem called "The Maker" is similarly cryptic:

And I am made,
ready
for the Sahara,
with a black ugly beak

that knows there's water
trembling in the cactus,
. . . .

ready
for the white hunter
heavy with ivory dream,
as he strokes his elephant-gun
and waits for the color of dawn.

(EAI, pp. 53-4)

For this reader "the white hunter/heavy with ivory dream" strongly recalls Conrad's *Heart of Darkness*. The poem is a good indication of Crusz's complexity. The allusions in the poems help him gain precision and compactness. However, as I stated earlier, as the allusions are not always picked from the Western literary tradition, they may be quite obscure to the Western reader. Or, sometimes, they may seem familiar but are given an unusual interpretation. The poem entitled "For the Winter Man" is a good example of his strategy. As the figure of the "Sun-Man" is associated with Crusz's Sri Lankan past, one must presume that the "Winter Man" here is the West personified:

For you
I bring gifts
of myrrh and cassia,
white ivory
heavy as boulders,
sweet blood of jambu.

I have truths
the color of bougainvillea,
parables plucked from sunsets,
eternal
as the core of the Buddha.

But winter's myths
have reached deep

into the marrow,
and there is now
no other way to the summer sun
but through a thick vein of ice.
Nothing will shake the discipline
of your season's clock,
melt the blue rinks of your eyes.
Like a puck
you'll remain silent hammered
to a corner
in winter's measured arena.

But when summer comes,
and the geometries of our moods
touch like tangents,
you'll no doubt accept these gifts
from the Sun-Man.

(EAI, p. 13)

The poem recalls the journey of the Magi but puts it in an entirely different context. For it also refers to ivory and to the Buddha. It is a wonderful rejoinder to Kipling's pessimism about the impossibility of the meeting of East and West, gaining its effectiveness from the Biblical allusion. The wise men had come from the East, the poet implies, and the West, he feels, needs another infusion of Eastern wisdom, "parables plucked from the Buddha's core." And parables are a favourite device of Crusz as well as other South Asian poets. Unlike the modern Western poet who prefers to speak in his own voice, the South Asian poets, raised on the *Pancatantra*, Aesop's and other traditional myths, parables and tales, use the parabolic structure quite frequently. Poems like "Sermon in the Forest" and "Kamala" are narrative poems, intertwined with references to other narratives. Many a time one comes across fables in the shorter poems as well:

I am crow
that lifts the last thimble
of water

from the pitcher's belly
with heaps of pebble,
sparrow free,
lightning-winged,
elephant smelling
the deep slope,
catching gun-sights in the wind.

(*EAI*, p. 53)

Another interesting aspect of Crusz's poetry, and one that he shares with other South Asian poets, is the use of references to artists and art forms of the Third World. "At Chalkie's Calypso Tent" pays tribute to the calypso artists of Port-of-Spain in rhythms that are as intoxicating as those of the calypso:

And bald Smiley,
champion of the poor,
your "Economy" song
came through so clear,
a solution for the arse
which could do well with water
instead of British toilet paper.

(*EAI*, p. 73)

Thus, the main referents in Crusz's poetry are from his Third World background. He is trying to communicate, through the use of these unfamiliar images, allusions, rhythms and structures, what it is to be an immigrant and a non-white in a society that is so dissimilar from that of one's origin. Unlike Michael Ondaatje, Crusz never suppresses those differences for the sake of gaining approval from the Canadian literary establishment. His "Immigrant's Song" (*EAI*) is not only an attempt to come to terms with his own past, it is also a heroic statement of poetic independence. While to his South Asian readers Crusz brings consolations from a fellow-immigrant who understands their reality and their loss, to other Canadians he brings a beneficial encounter with otherness, an insight into other ways of perceiving the world.

It is high time the mainstream, as it is called, took note of these voices from the outer periphery of Canadian life. Things as they stand now are pretty hegemonic. For example, Margaret Atwood's *The New Oxford Book of Canadian Verse in English* (1982) includes only two minority figures. However, in neither Michael Ondaatje nor Pier Giorgio Di Cicco does ethnicity become a major theme. Canadian Literature curricula at the universities are equally blank when it comes to the contributions of immigrant writers in general and non-white writers in particular. Such neglect is highly unfortunate for it encourages a rather narrow, ethnocentric view of literature—and, ultimately, of society itself—insensitive to unfamiliar voices and incestuously self-enclosed. The loss is especially deplorable in the case of immigrant writers from the Third World, writers who have been exposed to non-Western traditions of writing. Their poetry, if heard, could spark new areas of critical inquiry: the relationship of the poet to his tradition, the nature of differences between traditions, the culture-bound nature of poetic language and symbolism, and the nature of a poet's relationship with his audience. These, of course, are matters of technique. The voices of the coloured immigrant poets are important also because they report on Canadian society from a vantage point that is not available to a well-adjusted, native-born, "invisible" Canadian. They make their poetry out of what I would like to call the areas of silence in Canadian writing.

Interesting — visible, yet silent / invisible, yet heard

13. Narrating India:

Rohinton Mistry's 'Such a Long Journey'

The Nehru-Gandhi family has appeared as cast in many novels by writers of Indo-Pakistani background. The most well-known among these are Salman Rushdie's *Midnight's Children* and Nayantara Sahgal's *Rich Like Us*. Now Rohinton Mistry's *Such a Long Journey* picks up another thread from the rich fabric of narratives—imaginary and real—woven around India's unofficial royal family and tells us his version of a story that has been told and retold in India millions of times. For in India, the newspaper version is not the end of a story. It is recast and embroidered around roadside tea shops and family compounds every day. One person begins it and the others interject in between, speculating about the several possible ways the event could be narrativized. The event continuously calls for re-narrativizations and remains forever inconclusive. Thus many stories circulate about Jawaharlal Nehru's romance with Edwina Mountbatten, and with several other prominent Indian and Western women, about Sanjay and Rajiv's escapades as car thiefs in their youth, about Mrs Gandhi's visit to the grisly site of Sanjay's plane accident, supposedly to search for his watch that supposedly had information about the family's Swiss bank account, and about the Nagarwala case that provides the main plot for *Such a Long Journey*.

The best part of Mistry's novel for me is a preservation of this oral story-telling tradition of India. The novel inscribes these collectively known stories which do not make it into print, partly because they are apocryphal and partly because the inscriber must beware of libel suits. (Rushdie was sued by Mrs Gandhi and the case closed without coming to trial after her assassination.) These stories firmly place the novel in the company of those texts, currently labelled as "postcolonial," that have transformed the Western, individual-cen-

144

tred, "portrait"-oriented "novel" into a narrative form better able to place the individual within the collective. The social ethos in such texts comes across as a swarm of narratives which enmesh (rather than provide the background for) the individual narrative and help us grasp the individual characters' lives as they are lived in conjunction with the lives of *all* other human beings of that society. Perhaps Bakhtin's notion of "heteroglossia" comes close to describing what these texts attempt to do, but not quite close enough. For it only speaks of voices and not the stories these voices tell.

Here is how Mistry narrativizes these collectively known stories:

> But everyone knew that the war with China froze Jawaharlal Nehru's heart, then broke it. He never recovered from what he perceived to be Chou En-lai's betrayal. The country's beloved Panditji, everyone's Chacha Nehru, the unflinching humanist, the great visionary, turned bitter and rancorous. . . . His feud with his son-in-law, the thorn in his political side, was well known. Nehru never forgave Feroze Gandhi for exposing scandals in the government. . . . His one overwhelming obsession now was, how to ensure that his darling daughter Indira, the only one, he claimed, who loved him truly, who had even abandoned her worthless husband in order to be with her father—how to ensure that she would become Prime Minister after him.[1]

The insertion of such stories, the stories that "everyone knew," is what differentiates Mistry's novel from the "Victorian realist novel" that it has been compared to.[2] Instead of telling us about just "the moral growth of a complex and sympathetic character,"[3] it tells us about how his life is negotiated in the context of his total social environment.

And this total social environment, I insist, is real, not realist. That is, it attempts to make sense of actual historical events by narrativizing them, by extending them beyond the curtain of silence in which the official discourses have tried to enshroud them.

The actual event that Mistry has focused on is known in India as the Nagarwala case. In the winter of 1971, it was reported in the papers that the Head Cashier of the State Bank of India in Delhi had given six million rupees to Mr Nagarwala on the basis of a phone call from Mrs Gandhi who, he claimed, had asked him to take this great risk in the name of Mother India. After he had delivered the cash to Mr Nagarwala in a preassigned place, the Head Clerk had doubts about his act and went to the police. Mrs Gandhi denied that she had made any such telephone call and the Head Clerk was suspended. Nagarwala was arrested a few days later and confessed that he had mimicked Mrs Gandhi's voice.

The story has remained alive in the popular imagination because Nagarwala died in prison under suspicious circumstances, without ever coming to trial. Also, the high ranking civil servant who was investigating the bank's withdrawal and accounting practices met his death in a traffic accident on an isolated New Delhi road, giving rise to allegations of foul play. The mystery, thus, has never been satisfactorily resolved and Indian people often allude to the incident and fit in their own versions to the missing parts of the tale.

Mistry's version, like many other versions that I have heard, finds Mrs Gandhi guilty. He tells the tale from the perspective of Nagarwala who is cast as Major Bilimoria. He places him in a community in Bombay and weaves a tale which is both history and fabulation. He invents a friend for Nagarwala and narrates the events as they may be seen from his perspective. This friend, Gustad Noble, a bank clerk with three children and a wife, is the protagonist of the story. He is drawn in the concatenation of events when Bilimoria sends him ten lakh rupees which he asks him to deposit in a fictitious person's bank account. The novel describes his lower-middle-class life, his ambitions for his eldest son, his daughter's chronic stomach troubles, all against the backdrop of a Parsi neighbourhood. And it describes his friends and his work life at the bank since that's where the money is first deposited and then withdrawn. Given the factuality of the Nagarwala case, Mistry's inventions also take on the cast of believability. However, even a reviewer like Clark Blaise who knows quite a bit about India calls the tale a "set of paranoid inventions."[4]

Because Nagarwala was a Parsi, a minority community in India, the tale could only have been told by a Parsi. And as a tale told by a Parsi, it examines Indian society from the perspective of this minority community. And because Mistry is now a Canadian, a Canadian belonging to a minority community called South Asian, the narrative becomes double-coded. In the context of the constant debates in Canada around multiculturalism versus assimilation, passages like the following come wrapped in multiple ironies:

> The first time, Gustad was quite intrigued by the church and its rituals, so different from what went on in the fire-temple. But he was on his guard, conditioned as he had been from child-hood to resist the call of other faiths. All religions were equal, he was taught; nevertheless, one had to remain true to one's own because religions were not like garment styles that could be changed at whim or to follow fashion. (p. 24)

> What kind of life was Sohrab going to look forward to? No future for minorities, with all these fascist Shiv Sena politics and Marathi language nonsense. It was going to be like the black people in America—twice as good as the white man to get half as much. (p. 55)

> Darius said he would prefer five *Times of India*'s because his friends would make fun of the Parsi *bawaji* newspapers. Gus-tad would have none of that. "You should be proud of your heritage. Take the *Jam-E-Jamshed* or nothing at all." (p. 83)

Not only South Asian Canadians but other hyphenated Canadians who belong to minority communities will find their experiences reflected in these passages. And since many of them, particularly African-Caribbean, Indo-Caribbean and Indo-African Canadians, have histories of double migrations, the title *Such a Long Journey* will come for them with a double twist. For such double migrations, beginning in the eighth century for Parsis, are hard to fit into the popular critical paradigm of immigrant experience in Canada where the immigrant first suffers from nostalgia for "his" lost roots and then gradually settles down in "his" new Canadian home. This paradigm is too simple and excludes, perhaps deliberately, the dou-ble migration experiences of several communities in Canada, thereby decontextualizing their narratives.

To do full justice to *Such a Long Journey*, it is important to know the history of the Parsi community. The narrative is wedged in that history and to ignore it, or remain ignorant about it, is to misappropriate the text in the dominant paradigms of Canadian literary theory. Since the novel is not about new immigrants settling in the new Canadian environment, and, therefore, not fittable into "the new immigrant experience" paradigm, it has been fitted into the good old universalist paradigm where a morally upright character goes through experience that leads to his "moral growth" or helps him achieve "a deeper sense of his own humanity." [5]

The novel, in this interpretative frame, is about "the theme of the impermanence of all things" and addresses "important moral problems."[6] Heaven forbid that the novel also talks about life as it is lived under specific historical circumstances and demands that the cultural outsider pay attention to its cultural-historical specificity. The universalist paradigm ensures that these inane comments about "moral growth" and "the impermanence of things" will obviate the more urgently political agendas of the text. For if the Canadian reviewers paid attention to those, they might have to admit and explain the lack of such urgent agendas—political corruption, racism, rape of the environment, to name just three—in Canadian mainstream fiction and literary criticism. But the tone of the reviews suggests that political corruption is a Third World problem and has nothing to do with Canada.

The politics of apoliticalness embedded in the universalist theory employed in these reviews suggests that we single out the protagonist, Gustad Noble, from the totality of his environment and analyze him, his so-called "self," microscopically. This atomizing of the individual, however, is a liberal humanist reading practice and is grounded in the fiction of the sovereign Cartesian subject. In its pretension that such larger forces as geopolitical arrangements such as colonialism, neocolonialism, free trade, wars waged for territory and oil have nothing to do with the individual's life experiences, it promotes a conservative ideology in the guise of universality.

Even this individual-focused criticism, if done honestly, would take note of Gustad's multiple subject positions as an Indian citizen of Parsi ethnicity. For instance, he and his friends are highly suspicious of the machinations of the US. On the other hand, they regard the USSR with gratitude and affection for its tilt towards India. A reading that takes into account the world view of Gustad and his coworkers might lead to asking some hard questions about Canadian political attitudes regarding North-South relations. Similarly, the depictions of the fascist Shiv Sena might evoke parallels with the role of the Reform Party in Canada.

And so it is safe to focus on the "moving" portraits of these characters. That, it seems, is the highest approbation a Euro-American critic can grant to a text. It is worth pondering, however, what that word implies in terms of the critic's view of what is a literary text and what it does.

When the Euro-American critic comes down from the universalist heights and encounters the particular details of the text, "he" finds them "disgusting" and "repulsive."[7] The Parsi funeral rites have evoked this response from Westerners ever since the time of contact. Such epithets, I believe, only show the low level of tolerance for any kind of deviation from the Western norm. I think that the Parsi method of disposal of the dead is not only environmentally sound but also suggests a profound acceptance of the interconnectedness of all life. Count me among the "vulturalists."

The other details that remained with the reviewers were the none too pleasing smells of India. *Such a Long Journey*, Val Ross tells us, "is a tidal wave of humanity at its smelliest and most chaotic." It is "glistening brown pellets of ear wax, fingernail parings, sperm, cancers, diarrhea." Val Ross, in fact, does a reading not only of the novel but of the motives of the author as well: "Rohinton Mistry's need for peace, order and (relatively) good government—Canada, Brampton version—is understandable when you read his novel, *Such a Long Journey*. It is a tidal wave of humanity at its smelliest and most chaotic."[8] ~ why repeat this quote?

I do think that if these reviewers hold such condescending views of India, their readings of the novel will only reinforce their smug sense of Canadian (Western?) superiority. Here one has to ask whether the novelist has not—advertantly or otherwise—contributed to the possibility of such readings. But then, the great canonical Western text *The Portrait of an Artist as a Young Man* also has plenty of details about stench and, to use Val Ross's term, "bodily excrescences." However, that text is not talked about in such terms.

Ignorant and condescending as these reviews are, they no longer enjoy a total hegemony vis-a-vis how books will be read or interpreted. Val Ross does report Mistry's comment that an Indian critic described the novel as "the first book of fact-based fiction in the Indian literary tradition" (although I must interject and tell this Indian critic that that is not true. Certainly Nayantara Sahgal's *Rich Like Us*, published in 1985, is even more fact-based than *Such a Long Journey*). Obviously, readers in India and South Asians abroad will read from perspectives very different from the Eurocentric universalist ones.

While this South Asian reader has greatly appreciated the text's representation of the fecundity of India's oral narratives, I also must talk about my problems with the book. I found much of the humour—or attempt at humour—around sex and sexuality sexist. For instance, I wonder if the bank teller Laurie Coutino was named Laurie so that the author could tell us about the Parsi word for penis (lorri). Dinshawji's teasing of Laurie Coutino, asking her to play with his "sweet lorri" is sexual harrassment, not humour and the book, I suggest, would have been better without it. The only bawdy jokes that do fit in the text are the ones told in the bank canteen. The others seemed gratuitous and marred the book for me. The "Lokhundi Lund" tale, I think, ends up romanticizing the lives of Bombay's prostitutes since it is not juxtaposed against the actuality of their miserable lives. Again and again they are presented as sex machines, their sole role in the text as pleasure givers to the male. What about their poverty, exploitation, abduction in childhood and poor health?

Another part of the text that has bothered me is the portrayal of the female characters. While the men make money, tell tall stories, do adventurous things, the women indulge in superstition and black magic. Too much of the text is devoted to Miss Kutpitia and Dilnavaz conspiring about magic potions and spells. It is that part of the book that I found hard to swallow. After the initial portrayal of Dilnavaz getting up early to fill the water drums, the text tells us little about her life except for her silly attempts to "kill" Tehmul and her elaborate recipes for magic potions. Overall, the women's portrayals are stereotyped and unidimensional, whether it is Alamai, "the domestic vulture," or Miss Kutpitia or Dilnavaz or Laurie Coutino.

Given that *Such a Long Journey* is, after all, only his first novel, such flaws ought not to obscure Mistry's considerable achievement.

The novel, like his previous book, *Tales from Firozsha Baag,* is an impressive achievement. I do hope that as he gets a firmer grip on his art, his work will convey a more equitable balancing of the male and female aspects of our humanity.

14. 'Digging Up the Mountains':

Bissoondath's Doomed World

Digging Up the Mountains,[1] a collection of fourteen short stories by Trinidad-born Neil Bissoondath, adds another name to the sizeable list of Caribbean writers who have chosen Canada as their home.

Though Bissoondath came to Canada in 1973 at the age of 18, all but two stories deal with the Caribbeans. However, only two stories name Trinidad as a specific locale. In the rest of the stories the locale either remains nameless, leaving the reader to guess for himself through the help of suggestive clues such as names, topography or weather, or it is called "the island" or "the Caribbeans." I take this deliberate blurring of specific details as a suggestion on the writer's part that the situations and events described in these stories can pertain to all the Caribbean countries. Indeed, the blurb on the front jacket of the book would have us apply them to "the shifting politics of the Third World" in general.

The characters in these stories have one common link: they are in various stages of transit. The island, Mr Ramgoolam in "Insecurity" feels, is only a "temporary home" (p. 72) even though he was born there, nothing more than "a stopover." Vern's vision in "Veins Visible" can probably stand for the rootlessness of all the characters we encounter in the collection: "He saw the earth, as from space, streams of people in continuous motion, circling the sphere in search of the next stop which, they always knew, would prove temporary in the end" (p. 223).

Some of these characters have been forced to uproot themselves because of the legalized violence that, according to Bissoondath, is the way of life in the Caribbeans. The stories give the impression that the state violence is deliberately directed against the erstwhile prosperous East Indians. In the title story, Mr Hari Beharri's friends Rangee and Faizal die mysterious deaths while he himself gets

152

threatening phone calls in "lazy island drawl" (p. 7) and letters "typed askew on good quality papers, words often misspelt" (p. 7). Hari leads a paranoid existence, firing his gun at the mountains in the evening dusk and screaming at his would-be assailants, "Come, come and try" (p. 4).

The "black youths, wool caps pulled down tightly over their heads, impenetrable sunglasses masking their eyes" (p. 16), the Minister for State Security, "a big black man with a puffy face and clipped beard" (p. 7), and the policemen who are also black and wear the same "impenetrable glasses" arouse terror in Hari's mind in his various encounters with them. Hari finally decides to leave when his vandalized car is mockingly returned to him by the very policemen who had snatched it from him the day before.

Alistaire Ramgoolam in "Insecurity" is another prosperous East Indian who is planning to leave. He is cleverly smuggling out his money to Canada so that his son can buy a house in Toronto. Vernon in "Veins Visible" is also an East Indian who left out of fear for his life, leaving all his wealth behind him, and is now forced to paint houses in Toronto instead of hiring people to "paint our houses" (p. 214). These East Indians lead desperate, truncated lives in Toronto. Hari in "Veins Visible" dies in a drunken-driving accident while Vernon dreams about lying on the pavement with his torso severed from the rest of his body.

The stories carry hints of deep racial divisions in the West Indies. While "Digging Up the Mountains" presents the violence directly in terms of blacks as oppressors and East Indians as the oppressed, the hints in the other stories are more subtle. In "There Are a Lot of Ways to Die," Joseph goes back to his native island after six years of a life of "civility" in Toronto with the idealistic motive of "starting a business, creating jobs, helping my people" (p. 90). However, the twelve workers he has hired fail to show up the day the story opens because of rain, eliciting the comment from Joseph's wife: "These people like that, you know, gal. Work is the last thing they want to do" (p. 85).

However, along with the distrust for the racially different, there is also the phenomenon of self-hatred. The black priest at Joseph's school was "the terror of all students unblessed by fair skin and athletic ability" (p. 82). Sheila, "a ordinary-fifty-dollar-a-month-maid" in "Dancing" finds a similar contradiction: "Down there Black people have Indian maid and Indian people have Black maid. . . . Black people say, Black people don't know how to work. Indian people say, Indian people always thiefing-thiefing" (p. 188).

"Dancing" is the only story in which the narrator is a black person talking about herself and her family. The stories focus mainly on East Indian characters. Perhaps that is the material Bissoondath feels most comfortable with. However, this lack of representation of Black West Indians presents certain problems for a sensitive reader. As representatives of the state, the Blacks are shown as terrorizing and masochistic figures. In the only story dealing with Black characters in the lower walks of life, they are shown behaving most abominably. As previously mentioned, since Bissoondath has refrained from mentioning the names of particular countries, are we to presume that Blacks have wrested power everywhere and the East Indians are terrorized universally? Anyone familiar with Caribbean history knows that this is not necessarily so. In fact, works such as Michael Thelwall's *Harder They Come* claim just the opposite: that the majority Black population in Jamaica is oppressed by the coloured minority. I wonder if Bissoondath realized the implications of his method. The Caribbeans have a complex socio-cultural entity and lumping them together is bound to lead to distortions.

Whether it be the Caribbeans or the run-down slum houses in Toronto, or the vignettes of Europe and Japan that we see in "Continental Drift" and "The Cage," the world presented in the stories is uniformly bleak. There is no hope for redemption; individuals lead desperate, isolated lives in the absence of a viable community. "Christmas Lunch" describes a gathering of West Indians in a shabby house in Toronto by a narrator who is himself a stranger to the host and who has reluctantly joined the party at his friend's friends because the prospect of the festive lunch seems preferable to the other alternative: "a blustery Christmas day in a cold room with only a book for company" (p. 163). The lunch turns out to be a pathetic travesty of the proverbial Christmas spirit of joy and harmony as the little group fails to rise above its mean day-to-day existence.

A stranger-narrator is also employed in "A Short Visit to a Failed

Artist," another story about the East Indian Caribbeans in Toronto. These people, like the characters in "Christmas Lunch" and "Veins Visible," are leading fragmented, purposeless lives in a bottomless hell. However, I find it curious that the narrator, himself a West Indian, is a stranger to these characters and will probably never meet them again. One of the questions the reader might ask is whether this detached narrator is really the best vehicle for presenting these characters and whether he himself is not alienated from the joys and sorrows of this emigre community. The narrator's alienation and detachment, however, are presented without a trace of irony.

Only one short story, "Continental Drift," records a fleeting moment when human community is established. The narrator, a small-town Ontarian, suffering from "the incipient boredom" in his wanderings in Europe where prostitutes scream "Cheap fuck!" (p. 147) and empty syringes lie in the back alleys, is invited to share a meagre dinner by two young Spaniards who are looking for jobs in the French vineyards: "This one image," the narrator says, "will remain with me, will form of itself a glittering whole, will give value to an experience until now unsatisfactory" (p. 161). Once again, a reader might question why such moments of human fulfilment are not available in the Caribbeans and to the Caribbeans, especially since twelve out of the fourteen stories have to do with them. It seems a bit curious that though Europe figures only in one story it can still provide that elusive possibility of communion with one's fellow beings whereas all that goes on in the Caribbeans is "human madness" (p. 176) and "a certain stupidity" (p. 216).

If one had read these stories singly in magazines or heard them on radio broadcasts, one probably would not have noticed these disturbing meanings that arise out of juxtapositions. However, reading these fourteen stories together, one cannot but feel that certain judgements are being made without being openly articulated. The Caribbeans, we are told, have no future. The West Indians that we see in the stories have no redeeming qualities. Their lives lack even such basic civilities as love for one's family and regard for one's neighbours. Even the weather is uniformly rotten: it is rainy, foggy, steaming hot.

A corollary to this presentation is the view of Caribbean history that is voiced through one of the characters in "There are a Lot of Ways to Die": "our history does not lead anywhere. It's just a big, black hole" (p. 92). Since this view is not undercut by narrative irony or through utilization of history in other stories, one cannot but feel that it is supposed to be taken seriously. In the story, it is also reinforced by the symbolism of Pacheco House, a colonial ruin that had been built by "a crazy old man from Argentina" (p. 92) which is first declared a national monument and then allowed to go to ruin "with inexplicable murmurings of 'colonial horrors' " (p. 83). The view of the Caribbeans (or is it that of the entire Third World?) that emerges from these stories is strikingly similar to that expressed by V S Naipaul, Bissoondath's uncle: "a society without standards, without noble aspirations, nourished by greed and cruelty."[2]

Though it may seem unfair to generalize about the author's world view since the stories use either first person narrations or a disembodied narrative voice, the choice of subject matter, characters, symbolism, juxtapositions and narrative stance lead one to the inescapable feeling of total hopelessness. Political solutions are ridiculed. Left-wing phraseology such as "colonialism," "oppression," "American imperialism," etc. is especially under attack, at times in a most gratuitous manner and in flagrant disregard of the artistic unity of the story. While reading "The Revolutionary" one cannot help but conclude that it is not *a* Marxist that Bissoondath is attacking but all Marxists. The parody here is so exaggerated that it ceases to be funny: " 'Lo-lo-look,' he stammered, imploring belief, 'you ever heard about the Popular Insurrection Service Squad? Or the Caribbean Region Association of Patriots? No? Well, them's just two of the guerilla groups. Don't think I joking, man, I dead serious now'(p. 26)." One can only surmise which political organizations are being ridiculed as PISS and CRAP. The conclusion shows "the Revolutionary" tripping on his way out and with him go down not only the Marxist gods but also the future of Trinidad:

As he flapped his way to the door, the assistant librarian of the Future Train Movement—his head held high from pride or from the necessity of preventing his hair from crushing him— tripped over himself. Vladamir Ill Lenin, May-o, and the future of Trinidad went sprawling to the ground. (p. 29)

156

It is quite possible that one who does not share the author's biases will find it hard to read the stories as nothing more than aesthetic creations, to be savoured for their technical achievements exclusively. The present reader must admit to having experienced a constant sense of unease at the subtle and not so subtle ideological manipulations while reading the stories. It is not so much the violence and the corruption that I am disturbed by as by their removal from history and their presentation as the immutable condition of the Caribbeans. I cannot but disagree with the dust jacket blurb that the author has shown "a stout refusal to take sides."

Nevertheless, I do not mean to deny Bissoondath's narrative gifts. About seven of the fourteen stories are well written and manage to sustain the reader's interest through crisp dialogue, subtle manipulation of narrative suspense, interesting characterization and evocation of detail. "Digging Up the Mountains," "Insecurity," "Continental Drift" and "Counting the Wind" stand out especially. "Man as Plaything, Life as Mockery" and "The Cage" fail to work because of clichéd situations, all-too-familiar symbolism, wooden characters and long, descriptive narrative passages. Some stories fail to provide enough motivation or explanation to allow the reader to respond to the characters' dilemmas. "Veins Visible," "A Short Visit to a Failed Artist" and "An Arrangement of Shadows" are the weakest stories in the volume.

Judging by the better stories in the collection, Bissoondath has the potential to become an important voice in Canadian fiction.

15. 'A Planet of Eccentrics':
Begamudré's Fantastic India

Ven Begamudré's collection of short stories, called *A Planet of Eccentrics*,[1] signals its Indian content by employing the famous pillar of emperor Ashok as its cover adornment. Perhaps, unbeknown to the writer, and the graphic artist, the Ashok pillar is also the official seal of the government of India, and, for those from back home, brings back the association of the emblem with OIGS (On India Government Service), making the book somehow "official."

The perusal of the stories confirmed my suspicion that Begamudré's knowledge of India is gained from "official" sources and not from personal experience. There is much display of mythology, almost always forced, and this reader found herself constantly exclaiming, "Oh, no! Not again," as she encountered these too frequent allusions to the treasure trove of Indian myths and legends.

Although all the stories suffer from this desire on the author's part to add a layer of complexity to the narrative by sticking on these allusions, I will restrict myself to responding to the longest story in the collection, entitled "Samsara." It is written in the first person-narrative mode and recounts a newly-married, pregnant Canadian woman's first few weeks in a small village in Karnataka, called Debur Road. She is no longer Sara Davis but Saraswati Devi. She has given up her pants and shirts for nylon saris (I wish she wore cotton saris given how hot India is in June-July, the narrative time of the story) and she goes around the village barefoot (once again, my rational mind wanted to warn her of such dire consequences of walking barefoot as getting infected with ringworms and other parasites). She finds much symbolism in an unfinished bridge on the river which she hopes her soon-to-be-born son (why not a daughter? or a child?) will complete. And there are the regulation ferry man and the symbolic serpent figures under the bodhi tree where she will predictably get her enlightenment like the Buddha.

As I groaned under the weight of this heavy symbolic machinery being driven by a blue-sari-clad blue-eyed, red-haired Canadian woman from Kingston (intertextuality with Jeannette Turner Hospital?), what really got my goat was the revelation, forty-one pages into the story, six pages from the conclusion, that the title "Samsara" which I had taken to mean a profound comment on the world in the good old Indian tradition was not just about the Sanskrit meaning of *samsara* ("the world," "the flux," etc.) but about Sam and Sara: "Sam and Sara, Sara and Sam. Samsara. In some of my books, it's defined as the realm of existence; in others, rebirth according to the nature of one's karma" (p. 170).

I felt betrayed by this revelation. Is it supposed to be profound or comic? I have no idea. The inability of the story to signal the attitude a reader should adopt towards the narrator is an artistic failure of the first order. But as I have suggested earlier, I could not help but find Sara Davis alias Saraswati Devi one more stereotypical white woman gone overboard on India. However, if that was the idea, she should have been treated with a comic brush.

The other failure is the ultimate inability of the story to go anywhere. At the end of the story, although Sara claims that "my bridge is complete" (p. 175), I haven't got a clue why she thinks so and what has changed since the story began.

Nor do I know why Sara compares Sam, alias Shiamsundar, to not one but all the heroes in the *Ramayana* and the *Mahabharata*: "Sam is Yudhi-shthira, renowned as a ruler, son of the god of justice; Arjuna the warrior, high-minded, generous, handsome; Nakula, master of the horse; Saha-deva, learned in astronomy; even Bhima, the unrepentant slayer of foes. Above all, Sam is Rama, rightful king of Ayodhya" (p. 143). Later on, to hammer home an allusion, Sam's colleagues will be appropriately named Hanuman, Lakshman and Bharat. Why leave poor Shatrughan out, I ask:

"This looks very cozy," I say. He knows I mean this refuge, where he holds court like Rama, king of Ayodhya, with Lakshman playing the devoted brother Lakshmana; H Rao playing the monkey god Hanuman; Bharata playing the half-brother who acted as a regent while Rama searched for Sita. I will not play Sita, languishing in her captivity. (p. 163)

Forced profundity, alas, raises this reader's hackles. I like the subtle touch, not a poke in the eye. But, that, unfortunately, is what I kept getting. Begamudré seems distrustful of the reader's ability to take the hint and must spell it out, all the time.

Often, there isn't any real parallelism between the realistic surface and the juxtaposed myth. For instance, in "A Promise We Shall Wake in the Pink City After Harvest," Sinu, the village boy visiting Delhi to go through an arranged marriage, sits through the meeting with his in-laws staring at a calendar on the wall with the "picture of Jatayu, King of Vultures, battling Ravana, the many-headed King of Lanka" (p. 71). Now this is dissatisfying. On the one hand, it adds nothing to the story and, on the other, it is unrealistic. Calendars hanging on the walls of Indian homes portray more pleasant scenes from mythology. I, certainly, have never seen the type of calendar being described here.

The calendar is also a good example of Begamudré's lack of touch with India's social complexity. I found the "Pink City" and its companion stories difficult to swallow because their social details are all wrong. Such a calendar, for instance, will be passé in an upper-middle-class living room. (I assume they are upper middle class because the bride-to-be asks an ayah to bring in tea.) Then, generally, an upper-middle-class family which sends the daughter to an English-medium school is not likely to marry her off to a rural southerner with very little education. It also sounds unbelievable that the daughter does not know a word of Kannada. Or that the father speaks Kannada after a long gap only because his daughter's in-laws don't know Hindi or English. (I wondered why he wouldn't speak Kannada to his wife, who, again to my disbelief, is written out of the story though the word "parents" suggests that she is alive and right there.)

The companion story, "The Evil Eye," describing the death and the cremation of the bridegroom's father, is similarly incredible, for this reader. All guests invited to the wedding disappear as soon as he dies. That is absolutely impossible for me to believe. Anyone with any familiarity with Indian society knows that death in India requires as much of a gathering of friends and relatives as a birth or a marriage. However, Iruve's body is sent to the crematorium in the sole companionship of his son:

At noon, the city corporation van arrives to carry the corpse to the crematorium. Sinu climbs into the back alone, but even here he cannot find solitude. . . .

When Sinu returns to the house, his father-in-law says, "You are welcome to remain here until the immersion. We have no heating coil for your bath, but you may not go out now in any event. I see the chill air does not agree with you." (p. 55)

In real life, all the assembled male guests, or most of them, would be expected to accompany the body to the crematorium. In real life, the son would have lighted his father's pyre, not the attendant. And since the wedding ceremony suggested that these people were highly orthodox, in real life they would have performed rituals as elaborate as the ones for the wedding ceremony. And finally, given their affluent status, it seems very odd that they did not provide hot water for their son-in-law's bath. Or that they did not call a doctor to give him medication even though he was visibly sick.

But if the narrative were to remain faithful to patterns of behaviour expected from people in the Indian society, it would not go where Begamudré wants it to go. So, "The Evil Eye" first disposes of the father and then the son (who dies because of lack of medical attention), all supposedly to show that rituals to ward off the evil eye are powerless.

It would be futile to engage in a debate over the attempt by the mother-in-law to set her widowed daughter-in-law aflame. Isn't India known for what is called "dowry death"? However, I would still like to suggest that dowry deaths are a north Indian phenomenon and have an economic motive. Since the motive is to remarry for more dowry, a widow would be an unlikely candidate for a dowry murder. I also found it incredible that Janaki's parents don't come running to Debur Road after they hear of their son-in-law's death. Or, conversely, if we are to believe that Janaki's in-laws don't inform them about it, one would expect real life parents to get worried about the lack of news about their newly married daughter whose father-in-law died in their own home, and whose husband looked visibly sick when he left for his home with their daughter in tow. But, then, I have already mentioned how incredible their behaviour seemed to me. The stories fail to inform me if I am to see them as abnormally callous people or if they symbolise the total collapse of values in the Indian society, which I don't believe is true.

Other problems. If Debur Road is such a small community and if Janaki's uncle and aunt-in-law and their several children also live in the neighbourhood, one would expect them to make sure that Janaki's parents are informed of their daughter's widowhood and that she is treated properly. Her daily visit to the post office and her one-word conversation with the post master seem highly contrived for the very same reason. After all, one would expect that the post master would know English and so in real life, even if Janaki didn't know a word of Kannada (an improbability from my point of view), they could have conversed. The whole situation and the behaviour of the characters seemed absolutely unbelievable to me in the light of my knowledge of societal expectations in India.

None of Begamudré's characters come to life or behave as we expect real-life people to behave. Perhaps I am imposing realistic demands on a fiction which is really aspiring to "postmodernism," as signalled by its title. Postmodernism, as we all know, thanks to Linda Hutcheon, is about "Ex-centrics," or as the title story explains, in language reminiscent of Hutcheon: "To be eccentric . . . is to mean one is not situated in the centre, as an axis would be. To be eccentric is to mean one deviates from a perfect circle, and so the earth's motion around the son is eccentric" (p. 27).

I suppose the title would provide wonderful fodder to postmodernists about "ex-centricity" and marginality. However, marginality, as deployed in the postmodernist sense is not what these stories describe. The stories can best be described as vignettes of life in Debur Road, Nanjangud and Regina and a few other places in North America. A couple of them are science fiction and the first story, "Vishnu's Navel," takes place underneath the primordial sea. The people, whether real or mythological or science fiction, seem frozen on a canvas. There is a profusion of visual detail but skimpy narrative interest. All the stories come across as unconvincing in terms of the characters' motivation and behaviour. And, most dissatisfying to me, the India and the Indian people they describe are unreal.

It is not that Begamudré lacks the gift of story-telling. Many stories begin promisingly, particularly "Vishnu's Navel" and "Understanding Maya." However, Begamudré's obvious straining for effects spoils the game. He needs to learn to relax and trust the reader some more.

Begamudré's "Profile" in the December '91 issue of *Books in Canada* by Allan Casey informs us that he calls himself a "transcultural" writer. A "transcultural" writer owes it to the cultures he writes about that they are not exoticized or misrepresented. The Indians and the India represented in *A Planet of Eccentrics* remain, in the final analysis, unreal. Decontextualized to the nth degree, one is hard put to find any kind of normative categories against which to judge them. If Begamudré wishes to continue to write about India and people of Indian descent, it is imperative that he expand his background knowledge about them. Otherwise, he will once again end up excoticizing and demeaning them.

16. M G Vassanji's 'Uhuru Street'

In the early sixties, in a small town in central India, a Gujarati classmate of mine was married to a man who had come all the way from Nairobi, Kenya. For me and the other girls in my college, this man—tall, handsome, elegantly dressed, with an awesome Oxford accent—might as well have come down from outer space. And yet this arranged marriage, between a young Gujarati girl from Tikamgarh, India, and a prosperous Gujarati male from Nairobi, Kenya, remained an enigma to me. For no one explained to me that Indians had migrated to East and South Africa—as M G Vassanji narrates in his foreword to *Uhuru Street*[1]—even before 1498 and that the "discoverer" of India, Vasco da Gama, was indeed guided by two Indian sailors.

In fact, the history of these migrations, as well as India's centuries-long contact with Africa, remain obscured from the consciousness of the majority of Indians, including Indian historians. M G Vassanji's works, thus, are unique in exploring this history. His two novels, *The Gunny Sack* and *No New Land,* are motivated by a historic impulse: to make sure that his Shamsi community does not forget its history in its multiple migrations and their causes. Vassanji's recent collection of short stories, *Uhuru Street,* is permeated by the same desire: to record a history that has been ignored both by Indian Indians and African Africans.

In those two awkward phrases lies the dilemma Vassanji explores so poignantly in his works. His "Dar Indians," who are identified as Asian by native Africans and as Goans, Gujaratis, Cutchis, and Punjabis by themselves, tried to become Africans by donning Kaunda suits and spouting patriotic sentiments, and yet they failed. After several generations in Africa, they did not manage to become Africans. Vassanji's fiction is obsessed with exploring the reasons for this failure. And the honesty of his investigation brings out answers that are often unpalatable.

164

The importance of history for Vassanji's imagination is evident from the title of this collection. According to his short but absolutely indispensable foreword, "Once upon a time Uhuru Street was called Kichwele Street. The change marked a great event in the country. *Uhuru* means 'independence.' " The stories trace the lives of the members of a tightly knit community in the context of this momentous change in the history of Tanzania.

The stories in *Uhuru Street* can be divided into two categories: the ones that explore intracommunity relations and others that cast light on Indian-African relations. Many of the stories are part of a sequence and are woven around the lives of a fatherless family where the narrator's mother runs a general store on Kichwele/Uhuru Street with the help of her five children. We meet the members of this family and their circle of friends and relatives in stories like "Ali," "Alzira," "For a Shilling," "The Relief from Drill," "The Sounds of the Night," and "Leaving." Together, these stories become a family portrait and resonate intertextually—the reader coming to each story with incremental knowledge. Since even the minor characters recur often, some of them recalled from Vassanji's novels, the reader has a sense of inhabiting a familiar universe. Vassanji's fiction, thus, is heading in the direction of that of writers like Faulkner, Hardy and Margaret Laurence whose fictional universe is a densely patterned fabric and whose nuances can be fully appreciated only if the reader is committed to the entire *oeuvre*.

The stories in *Uhuru Street* are not focused on an individual's "private" life or a personal learning experience but on the individual enmeshed first within the family and then within the larger Asian community whose interactions with the African and European communities are severely limited due to the hierarchies of the colonial order. The Europeans here appear as celestial beings, incomprehensible and inaccessible, objects of a reverential gaze. Princess Margaret, dressed in white, arrives "as if an angel had descended from the sky. And beside her, in his tasselled black and gold ceremonials, the Governor, Sir Philip Morrisson—a name whose each syllable we had learnt to pronounce with mystical awe."

The Africans, on the other hand, are beneath the Indians. While they appear as domestic servants and menial workers in the stories set in pre-independence Tanzania, the roles are reversed after independence. "Ali," the story about the African servant of the narrator's family, is written with a stark honesty that denotes Vassanji's determination to face history squarely. Ali's sexual attraction for Mehroon, the narrator's sister, can never be acknowledged publicly. His desire to marry her one day is impossible to fulfil. The taboo on sexual relations between Indians and Africans is also explored in "Breaking Loose." A romance develops between an African professor and an Indian student despite tremendous barriers. I found it one of the sweetest stories in the collection, positive and forward-looking, whereas others are haunted by the inevitability of the departure of Indians from Tanzania.

And yet, despite this massive outward migration, there are exceptions. "Ebrahim and the Businessman" describes an anomalous Asian who, because his own community shunned him, opens up to the African community and ends up as a minister in the government. However, one wonders if he too will be pushed out as a similar character—Jamal in *No New Land*—was pushed out, since the two characters' careers are so similar. Given the historic reality and the scramble for emigration described in the stories, the return of the narrator of "All Worlds Are Possible Now" from Canada to reclaim his African heritage reads more like a fantasy than a realistic portrayal and, therefore, generates ironies that are perhaps unintended.

The ambivalent role of Indians in Africa is brought out most clearly in "The Driver." Idi, the driver, is upset about having "to urinate against the stained, yellow back wall" because the employer's wife won't let him use the household toilet: "Wait, he had thought then, smarting from the insult. We'll have our day." It is only after reading about these unsettling relations, in stories like "Ali," "The Driver," and "Breaking Loose," that the reader can grasp the intensity of hatred that leads an African bank clerk to rape and murder a Canada-bound Indian woman in "What Good Times We Had."

Just as the title of this story about the murdered woman is ironic, the entire collection reverberates with subtle ironies. Servants become masters and masters abscond. Severely guarded virginity that had felt outraged even at a marriage proposal by an African chief is brutally violated, and Idi's thoughts —"We'll have our day"—turn out to be prophetic. Perhaps the most ironical and most poignant story is "All Worlds Are Possible Now," where the return of the narrator, lest it become sentimental, is parodically intertexualized and thus becomes a literary trope. A German passenger on the plane, "an expert on literature from our part of the globe," compares the narrator's situation with that of returning literary heroes: "Yes, yes. I would like to recommend a novel. It's called *Time Reversal*. Yes?. . . It's about a young man—like you—who returns to his home country, or tries to, but he dies on his way back. Yes?"

Although the narrator refuses the German expert's analysis and declines "to live according to the dictates of irony," or "become slave to an aesthetic," the reader cannot but fail to notice another irony: that the creator of this returnee narrator has himself left Africa like thousands of others of his community. Expatriate writers' fiction is replete with fantasies of return and Vassanji is no exception.

Overall, *Uhuru Street* is a densely textured, carefully crafted work. Practically all the stories retained my interest, although some, like "The Beggar" and "The Sounds of the Night," remained mysterious as to their intent. Vassanji has a remarkable capacity for creating a complex narrative pattern with seemingly simple details of day-to-day life. And yet, hidden in these same mundane details are tough questions about history, colonialism, and the ambiguous role of Indians as a comprador group whose dual role as the colonized and as collaborators makes it hard to portray their situation in the binary opposition of colonizer/colonized prevalent in postcolonial criticism.

Some reviewers have compared *Uhuru Street* to V S Naipaul's *Miguel Street*. I don't think any two books are so diametrically opposed as these two in terms of their attitudes towards the land and the people they represent. While *Miguel Street* ends with what can be called a "release" of the protagonist narrator from his despised surroundings and migration to the seat of the empire, *Uhuru Street*'s last story is about the return of the native. If the titles of the two books indicate an intertextuality, *Uhuru Street* can be considered an oppositional rewriting of its predecessor insofar as it rejects the *bildungsroman* pattern of *Miguel Street* and undertakes a radical investigation of historical events of the last two centuries as they have moulded the life of a community.

It is the unabashedly communitarian or "ethnic" bent that identifies *Uhuru Street* as a work belonging to the category called South Asian Canadian literature, and to which it makes an important contribution. It tells a story that has never been told before, and Vassanji can be credited for having discovered a crucial piece in the jigsaw puzzle of South Asian history, a history that should interest other Canadians as well, since it is inextricably tied to Canada's role in the global drama of colonialism.

It is unfortunate that this significant book has been given such an inappropriate cover. For instance, even though the book is set in Africa and deals with African realities, no African face is included. Instead, we have Mick Jagger and Indian movie stars —Om Prakash and Neetu Singh—pictured on the cover. What bothered me no end was that while Mick Jagger's photograph was reprinted with permission, no such courtesy is extended to the Indian movie stars whose faces will not be recognized by most Canadians. Why is it that Third World resources are free for exploitation by the first worlders, whereas their own resources are strongly guarded by patents and copyright laws?

I do hope that this inadequate cover is not an indication of the future fate of *Uhuru Street*, in which its so-called nuances and complexities will be savoured in the name of a universality at the cost of its contextual affiliations. That will be the ultimate irony for a writer whose protagonist narrator fumes at having been pigeonholed as "a slave to an aesthetic."

17. Writing from a Hard Place:
The African Fiction of M G Vassanji

M G Vassanji's career provides a good example of what happens to writers who do not fit into the prevailing paradigms of literary theory. Or who do not write from the right location. Although his first novel *The Gunny Sack* won the Commonwealth Prize in the African region (when it should really have been considered in the North American region), critical attention to the novel has been minimal, or almost nonexistent in Canada. The later books, *Uhuru Street* and *No New Land,* although published in Canada, have not aroused critical interest either. In short, he is not hot in Canada.

As far as his lack of visibility in Canada is concerned, Vassanji has himself written about how Canadian literary establishment marginalizes non-white writers by categorizing them as "immigrants": "The term is . . . used somewhat condescendingly to describe a transition stage of no vital importance, a stage of growing up which we all have to go through before maturity."[1] He complains of the Canadian critics who hold that "a writer matures when he begins to talk of his 'Canadian experience'."[2]

The truth of Vassanji's complaint is evident from the fact that Frank Davey can write him off in a footnote in his *Post-National Arguments.* Davey excuses himself from considering Vassanji, and Nino Ricci and Rohinton Mistry, by claiming that their novels "contain few if any significations of Canada or of Canadian polity."[3] Such an exclusion is highly ironic given the title of Davey's book which declares that Canadian literature needs to be studied beyond the confines of nationalism.

The fact of the matter is that writers perceived as "ethnic" remain excluded from Canadian literature anthologies and Canadian literature courses. The common-sense assumptions about Canadian identity and Canadian content continue to rule invisibly even though they have been challenged quite vigorously by critics such as Margery Fee, Robert Lecker and Davey himself.

While these nationalist assumptions, grounded in an exclusion-ary and racist view of Canadian identity make Vassanji's work invisible in Canada, where he lives and writes from, he has not been considered an African writer either, despite the claim on the cover of *The Gunny Sack* that it is "Africa's answer to *Midnight's Children*." It is not that he is rejected by his homeland, i.e. Tanzania, where he had a very warm reception when he visited a couple of years ago and where many people *had* read and enjoyed *The Gunny Sack*. If he is not considered an African writer, it is because the criticism on African literature is produced in Europe and North America, mostly by white and African American critics who perceive Africa in ho-mogeneous and essentialist terms. So even though the Tanzanian academics responded to Vassanji's work warmly, their working conditions prevent them from publishing as critics. (Vassanji in-formed me that their poor working conditions had led many Tanza-nian academics to supplement their income by turning to farming. Another grave problem they face, along with other African academ-ics is the dearth of indigenous publishing outlets.)

The postcolonial theorists who teach and write about African literature have produced a homogenized "native," whose voice is authentically recoverable in the writings of canonized writers like Achebe, Soyinka and Ngugi. As I have suggested elsewhere,[4] this criticism makes naive assumptions about the commonalities be-tween postcolonial societies and postcolonial literatures. And it often sees the literary text as an expression of the aspirations of an entire people. These critics often use the singular noun "native" to speak of an entire nation, and at times, the entire non-Western world. The "resistance" of this native to the colonizer is the master narrative that postcolonial theorists have produced and continue to produce.

The focus on "resistance," on "writing back to the centre," has valorized the works that represent the great drama of national struggles and the corollary search of the nationalist bourgeoisie for a national identity. These works, it is assumed, speak of a united "people" whose heroic struggle finds a voice through the writer. Thus we have works like *Untouchable*, *Nectar in a Sieve* and *Kan-*

thapura where the voices of upper-caste and upper-class writers speak for those less privileged and are received as though they spoke of all Indians. Although these works suggest that there are no oppressor-oppressed relations among the colonized themselves, that there are no Brahmins and no untouchables, all becoming equalized in the great wave of the freedom movement, one would like the postcolonial critics to interrogate such a claim rather than tout them as authentic representations.

This homogenizing of the "native" has occluded both diversity and conflict. It has constructed national spaces as homogeneous, both culturally and racially. Thus, the Caribbean and Africa are assumed to be black just as India is assumed to be Hindu. The authentic culture that the colonized people of these places supposedly yearn for is also spoken of in the singular. And thus we have a scenario where nationalism is ritualistically denounced and yet reproduced silently through the way writers are categorized and spoken of.

As the subaltern historian Ranajit Guha has pointed out, nationalist narrativising of history followed a similar path. The nationalist historians have projected the nation as far back as possible and history marches forward predictably towards the great culmination of the overthrow of the colonizers by the heroic efforts of a few chosen leaders. So I was told about the great betrayers of the nation like Mir Jafar and Jaychand and the great heroes like Shivaji and Rana Pratap. These people were presented by my high-school history books as "betraying" or "defending" a nation called India way before the modern nation state by that name came into being.

This monolithic narrative taught to me in large doses wiped out a multiple of histories. We did not learn about the histories of our country's diverse communities. Nor did we learn about our local environments. Although I lived in a town where a huge fort looks down on the inhabitants, our local history was not a subject of study.

In my review of Vassanji's *Uhuru Street*, I have written about a girl in my home town who was married off to a man who came all the way from Kenya. While I attended the ceremony and heard talk about her going to live in Africa, I did not know about the presence of sizeable communities of Indian people in Africa and I assume that my elders did not know either since they did not answer my queries as to how this Indian-looking person had come from Africa.

When I remember this significant event from my adolescence, I am struck by the insularity of our communities. The girl who got married was a Gujarati and the two or three Gujarati families in our north Indian town probably knew all about Indians in Africa. However, the rest of us did not know and were not told.

Similarly, my first encounter with Indo-Caribbean people occurred in Toronto, in the roti shops and on the subways. Their faces suggested to me that they were somehow related to me and yet I did not know how. And lest my ignorance be construed as my personal fault, I have yet to meet a recent arrivee from India who knows anything about the nineteenth-century migrations from India to the Caribbean.

The point I am driving at is that these migrations of Indian people in the wake of the British empire have been forgotten as of no relevance to India and Indian history. I was a student of geography and was taught about Africa from books written by white geographers with pictures of naked pygmies standing in front of their grass huts. So, while my history books did not tell me about the centuries-long connections between India and Africa, my geography books told me about an Africa that was inhabited by "savages."

Vassanji's *The Gunny Sack*, published in 1989, was my first window into the Indian presence in Africa. Rather than reading it as "Africa's response to *Midnight's Children*," as the blurb on the front cover suggests, I read it as an Indian rewriting of *Heart of Darkness*. It breaks a great silence and speaks from a place and about things that we Indians have forgotten. For it is not a narrative of heroic deeds. Nor is it a narrative of oppression and victimization, the narratives privileged these days. It is a narrative about mundane things, about day-to-day lives of people who did not "resist" but colluded with the empire. And to the extent that it does not position itself as the voice of "the colonized," it is written from a hard place.

When one is positioned as the wronged party and can write about generations of oppressions, it is a position of moral rightness. And there is nothing more powerful than this kind of writing. It is the position that rightly belongs to those Fanon called "the wretched of the earth." It is the position that belongs to African Americans and the aboriginal people in North America. It is the position that Afro-Caribbeans and Indo-Caribbeans seem to be fighting about to determine who has suffered the most.

But how does one write if one belongs among the oppressors rather than the oppressed? What does one write about if one cannot point a finger at someone else? That is, how and what does one write about if the story one has to tell is not about epic heroes and great deeds? In fact, how does one write if history has positioned one as a Mir Jafar or a Jaychand?

Those are the questions Vassanji must have had to answer in writing *The Gunny Sack*. And in answering them, he has written about people, who, like my mother and father and uncles and aunts, did not go to jail or march in rallies during the Indian indendence struggle. Lives of unheroic people require an understated style that stays clear of lyricisms and tragic effects and aspires to a flat, documentary stance. That style is Vassanji's trade mark in all his three works of fiction.

Vassanji's subjects are shopkeepers or "Baniyas."[5] *The Gunny Sack* painstakingly describes almost hundreds of shopkeepers and what they do. Meet Mzee Pipa:

> Scrooge in Kariakoo. His hands would be in continuous motion. He would put a handful of spice or gum on a piece of square paper, then fold it rapidly, twice, to make a cone, then a third time, and finally tuck the remaining edge in and throw the finished packet into a basket. It would fetch ten cents from some African woman out to buy the day's groceries. . . . Drop by drop, they said, you can fill an ocean. With clink after patient clink of ten-cent coppers in the cashbox he had acquired his wealth. (p. 101)

As Robert Gregory writes in *India and East Africa*,[6] since writing in ancient India was under the control of Brahmins, they concentrated on "religious subjects, [and] did not deign . . . to describe the activities of the Vaisyas, among whom were the shipwrights and traders engaged in Indian Ocean commerce." *The Gunny Sack*, I may say, is the first book from the perspective of the Baniya community, a community about whom negative phrases abound in the Indian languages that I know, namely, Hindi, Punjabi and Bundelkhandi.

Baniyas, according to these aphorisms are miserly, cautious, uncultured and cowardly. Mahatma Gandhi, of course, was an exception.

Also, Baniyas are perceived as Hindus. Vassanji, by claiming that title for his syncretic Muslim community deconstructs another stereotype. His shopkeepers are Bohras, Memons, Khojas, Ismailis, and, his fictional Shamsis. All this variety is very instructive to me as a Hindu Indian reader who has not known about the diversity of Indian Muslims. Vassanji fills in these details with the precision of an anthropologist. "Take the name Yusufali Adamjee, outside the small store that sells stationery (among other things) in Kaboya. A name that immediately identifies a Gujarati Muslim of a certain sect from Surat, who traces his ancestry in Arabia" (p. 219). As I read further about Yusufali calling Salim Juma in and inquiring about his kins, I couldn't help but chuckle. For it brought back memories of how my elders established relationships and placed people.

One of the many aspects of the book that gives it the documentary, antiheroic feel is its strategy of providing hundreds of such little sketches of hundreds of "dukawallas," in Dar, in Nairobi, in Mombasa, in Zanzibar, and a large number of small towns and hamlets of east and central Africa. Wherever you go in East Africa, there is a duka and a dukawallah it seems.

Vassanji uses two temporalities, the mythic and the calendrical. The mythic time scheme suggests that Indians had been going to the east coast of Africa for centuries. They were there before the colonial powers got interested in Africa. They were there to trade in slaves, ivory, cloves and hides. Now that was another surprise to me. As Gregory says, "The history of India's relationship with Africa has received very little attention from scholars concentrating on India, Africa, or the British empire."[7] I was, for instance, shocked to read that India imported slaves from Africa and continued to import them right up to the nineteenth century. It is only in the light of this new knowledge that the "Slave Dynasty" that I had read about in my high school history books, and the fact that neither the book nor my history teacher explained why it was so called, begins to make sense.

Vassanji's narrator, Salim Juma, records slavery and Indian participation in the institution without judging it:

On a clear morning you could just about see in a distant haze the land mass that was the continent of Africa. In the evenings some saw the fires that slavers made as signals to incoming dhows. Every morning the harbour was abustle, with dhows setting off for the mainland. Traders, hunters, guides, explorers, porters, immigrants and civil servants left every day for that sleeping, beckoning land mass, waved off by well wishers and onlookers. A year after his arrival at Zanzibar, Dhanji Govindji landed at Bagamoyo. While the Europeans, the hunters and porters, the seasoned Swahili traders, went inwards to seek greater fame or fortune, my forebear joined a small caravan going southwards on the slave route. (p. 9)

Salim's great-grandfather buys a slave from his fleeing German customer in 1915, ten years after slavery had been technically abolished under German rule: "The retainer, as the German would explain, was born in 1903 and technically was still a slave" (p. 47). And there is Bibi Taratibu, the female slave, whom Dhanji Govindji buys for thirty rupees in 1885, and makes a note of the purchase in his diary.

It is this purchasing of sexual services that inspires Salim to utter one of the rare hyperboles in the novel: "Matamu. . . . It is the town where my forebear unloaded his donkey one day and made his home. Where Africa opened its womb to India and produced a being who forever stalks the forest in search of himself. It is where Bibi Taratibu, given as a gift for cold nights, was so used and discarded, and then disappeared" (pp. 39-40). Here Govindji's transgression becomes a metaphor of national encounters. India's relationship with East Africa is seen in terms of sexual domination. The feminine "Mother India" of the nationalist Indian is transformed into a seducing male.

The metaphor really got my attention as India has always been described in feminine images, both by the nationalists and the colonizers. The metaphor compels me to read *The Gunny Sack* as an allegory of exploitation. The "using" and "discarding" of Bibi Taratibu becomes a trope for Indians' relationship to their adopted land.

The Gunny Sack, I think, is about guilt and betrayal. About the original sin of abandonment committed by Dhanji Govindji. About the betrayal of Mary's son to the British police by Juma, the Mary who had treated Juma as her own son. And finally, it is about Salim abandoning Tanzania for Toronto. Salim carries the accumulated guilt of several generations of his family and judges them as he judges himself. It is not only Mary "whose memory we now carry branded forever in our conscience . . ." (p. 78), but several women, metonymically representing Africa, who torment Salim's imagination.

Salim has an interesting subject position, quite contradictory to what I hear at the parties of Asian Africans in Toronto. They see themselves as victims who were hounded out of Africa. Vassanji, on the other hand, insists that what happened in Uganda is not what happened in Kenya and Tanzania. All his three books have characters who return to Tanzania. *The Gunny Sack*, too, ends with Salim resolving to go back to his wife in Tanzania:

> The running must stop now, Amina. The cycle of escape and rebirth, uprooting and regeneration, must cease in me. Let this be the last runaway, returned, with one last, quixotic dream. Yes, perhaps here lies redemption, a faith in the future, even if it means for now to embrace the banal·present, to pick up the pieces of our wounded selves, our wounded dreams, and pretend they're still there intact, without splints, because from our wounded selves flowers still grow. (pp. 268-269)

Salim wants to reclaim Africa, to expiate his family's, and by extension, India's wrong done to Africa. Even though Dar voices call him "one of the exploiter class, a dukawallah, mere agents of the British, these oily slimy cowardly Asians" (p. 228), he decides to go back.

But the book ends here, with the decision to go back. The narrative of Salim back in Tanzania awaits to be written. Perhaps it cannot be written by a writer who has himself left Tanzania and lives in Toronto. The narrative about the returned Salim can only be written by an Asian African who really returned. Or someone who never left. That would be the narrative of redemption.

Will such a narrative ever be written? Can settlers and colonizers live down their past? For as Salim admits, Indians in Africa were that. Salim quotes Harry H Johnston's words:

> This beautiful fertile country, let it become the America of the

Hindu, a British governor had pronounced at the turn of the century. He had invited Indian dukawallahs to help open up the interior for trade, to buy African cotton for British ginneries and sell British-made cloth and shirts back to the African. (p. 244)

This, too, is a chapter of Indian history that was not known to me. That there was an influential lobby in India that wanted East Africa to become an Indian colony. It included prominent leaders like the Aga Khan, G K Gokhle, Sir Pherozeshah Mehta, and Sarojini Naidu. It is astounding to read A M Jeevanjee, a prominent Asian African merchant, claiming, in language reminiscent of today's Vishwa Hindu Parishad, that East Africa should be annexed to the Indian empire because "[i]t had been an Asiatic kingdom in ancient time." He dreamed that "East Africa will assuredly become a Second India in no time"[8] provided the British government followed his proposal to open up East Africa to the Indians.

A M Jeevanji, Gregory's book tells me, donated the famous marble statue of Queen Victoria in Nairobi that was unveiled in 1906 by the Duke of Connaught. Although Vassanji comments on the Asians' allegiance to the British in all three of his books, this passage from *No New Land* is especially *apropos*:

The idea of empire was relinquished slowly in the Asian communities. Right up until independence, letters would arrive addressed ostensibly to someone in "British East Africa." The Asians had spawned at least two knights of the empire in their slums, they had had Princess Elizabeth in their midst, greeted Princess Margaret with a tumultuous welcome. They spoke proudly of Churchill and Mountbatten, fondly of Victoria.[9]

The nationalistic narratives of history have preferred to gloss over such complicities. They are nothing to write about in comparison to the Jullianwalla Bagh massacre, the Quit India movement, the Salt March and other such major occurrences. However, the heroic narratives of "resistance" that nationalist historiography constructs obscure the fact that the colonizers could not have been able to rule without the concurrence of at least some of the ruled. I would agree with C A Bayly that "Indians remained . . . active agents and not simply passive bystanders and victims in the colonial India."[10]

Vassanji's narratives speak from that space of collusion and collaboration. His Indians admire the British might, and he unabashedly brings it out, however embarrassing it sounds. While many dates are mentioned in the three books, 1947, the year of India's independence and partition, is not one of them. It does not seem to have caused a ripple in the consciousness of the dukawallahs. And as to the Maji Maji war and the Mau Mau movement, the Asians portrayed in *The Gunny Sack* side with the colonizers.

But it is not only the Asians who betrayed Africa. Vassanji writes of conflicting interests and divided loyalties. He shows how the Germans in East Africa used Africans to control fellow Africans. "The Germans employed barbarous askaris, the Nubians, who had no qualms opening up the bellies of women with child. The Masai, the rumours said, were already on their way from the north" (p. 16).

When Amina, Salim's African sweetheart accuses him of having conveniently forgotten that his ancestors "financed the slave trade," he answers: "If mine financed the slave trade, yours ran it. It was your people who took guns and whips and burnt villages in the interior, who brought back boys and girls in chains to Bagamoyo. Not all, you too will say . . . " (p. 211).

Vassanji, then, refuses to participate in the heroic narratives of freedom struggles. Unlike many other African and Indian novelists, he refuses to write about "the people." Instead, he writes about the distinct ethnic groups, of the Arabs, the Mangati, the Swahili, the Masai, the Khoja, the Goan, the Bohra, the Bhatias and on and on the list goes. Perhaps he writes that way because of who he is. Perhaps he, too, would have written of the great freedom struggles had history bequeathed him a less ambiguous perch. But what is certain is that his special take on the master narratives of freedom struggles reminds us that much too often they wipe out embarrassing realities whose memories might make us less self-righteous.

Notes

INTRODUCTION

1. Arun Mukherjee, *Towards an Aesthetic of Opposition: Essays on Criticism and Cultural Imperialism* (Stratford: Williams-Wallace, 1988).
2. Arun Mukherjee, "A House Divided: Women of Colour and American Feminist Theory," in Constance Backhouse and David Flaherty, ed., *Challenging Times: The Women's Movement in Canada and the United States* (Montreal and Kingston: McGill-Queen's University Press, 1992), pp. 165-174, n. 309-312.
3. Arun Mukherjee, "Right Out of 'Herstory': Racism in Charlotte Perkins Gilman's *Herland* and Feminist Literary Theory," in Himani Bannerji, ed., *Returning the Gaze: Essays on Racism, Feminism and Politics* (Toronto: Sister Vision, 1993), pp. 131-143.
4. Janet Mancini Billson, " 'Challenging Times': Complexities of Feminism and the Women's Movement," *Canadian Review of American Studies* Special Issue, Part II (1992), p. 323.
5. Chinua Achebe, "An Image of Africa: Racism in Conrad's Heart of Darkness," in *Hopes and Impediments: Selected Essays 1965-87* (London: Heinemann, 1988), pp.1-2.

CHAPTER 1

1. Arun Mukherjee, *Towards an Aesthetic of Opposition: Essays on Literature, Criticism and Cultural Imperialism* (Stratford: Williams-Wallace, 1988).
2. Arun Mukherjee, *The Gospel of Wealth in the Modern American Novel: The Rhetoric of Dreiser and Some of His Contemporaries* (London, Sydney: Croon Helm, 1987).
3. Michael Thelwell, *Harder They Come* (New York: Grove Press, 1980).
4. Alice Walker, *Meridian* (New York: Pocket Books, 1976).

CHAPTER 3

1. Chinua Achebe, "Thoughts on the African Novel," in Rowland Smith, ed., *Exile and Tradition: Studies in African and Caribbean Literature* (New York: Africana Publishing Company, Halifax, NS: Dalhousie University Press, 1978), p. 4.
2. Victor Ramraj, "V S Naipaul: The Irrelevance of Nationalism," *World Literature*

Written in English 23, 1 (1984), 195.

3. Ramraj, 187.

4. Helen Tiffin, "Commonwealth Literature and Comparative Methodology," *World Literature Written in English* 23, 1 (1984), 28.

5. Northrop Frye, "Across the River and Out of the Trees," *Divisions on a Ground: Essays on Canadian Culture* (Toronto: Anansi, 1982), pp. 31-32.

6. R N Egudu, "J P Clark's *The Raft*: The Tragedy of Economic Impotence," *World Literature Written in English* 15, 2 (1976), 297-304.

7. Haydn Moore Williams, "Strangers in a Backward Place: Modern India in the Fiction of Ruth Prawer Jabhvala," *Journal of Commonwealth Literature* 6, 1 (1971), 63.

8. Williams, p. 54.

9. The following comments of Achebe are quite apropos here: "The other day one of them spoke of the great African novel yet to be written. He said the trouble with what we have written so far is that it has concentrated too much on society and not sufficiently on individual characters and as a result it has lacked 'true' aesthetic proportions. I wondered when this truth became so self-evident and who decided that (unlike the other self-evident truth) this one should apply to black as well as white." Achebe, "Where Angels Fear to Tread," G D Killam, ed., *African Writers on African Writing* (London: Heinemann, 1973), p. 6.

10. T W Clark, "Introduction," *Pather Panchali: Song of the Road* by Bibhutibhushan Banerji, trans. T W Clark and Tarapada Mukherji (London: Allen & Unwin, 1968), pp. 15-16.

11. I believe that we in the Third World have a hard time with the concept that an individual can either single-handedly change his destiny or is responsible for what happens to him. I cannot forget that the life of my family was inexorably changed by the creation of Pakistan.

12. Interview with P A Egejuru, *Towards African Literary Independence: A Dialogue with Contemporary African Writers* (Westport, Conn.: Greenwood Press, 1980), p. 106.

13. Raymond Williams, *The English Novel: From Dickens to Lawrence* (Frogmore: Paladin, 1974), p. 143.

14. Jean E Kinnard, *Victims of Convention* (Hamden, Conn.: Archon Books, 1978).

15. R K Narayan, "English in India," in John Press, ed., *Commonwealth Literature: Unity and Diversity in a Common Culture* (London: Heinemann, 1965), p. 123.

16. J P Clark, quoted in Abiola Irele, *The African Experience in Literature and Ideology* (London: Heinemann, 1981), p. 36.

17. S K Desai, "Arun Kolatkar's *Jejuri*: A House of God," *Literary Criterion* 17, 1 (1982), 48.

18. Meenakshi Mukherjee, "Macaulay's Imperishable Empire," *Literary Criterion* 17, 1 (1982), 38.

19. Fredric Jameson, *The Political Unconscious: Narrative as a Socially Symbolic Act* (Ithaca, NY: Cornell University Press, 1981), p. 85.

20. S C Harrex, "R K Narayan: Some Miscellaneous Writings," *Journal of Commonwealth Literature* 13, 1 (1978), 71.

21. S C Harrex, "A Sense of Identity: The Novels of Kamala Markandeya," *Journal of Commonwealth Literature* 6, 1 (1971), 65, 67. Meena Shirwadkar in her *Images of Woman in the Indo-Anglian Novel* (n.p.: Sterling Publishers, 1979) notes that several male Indian critics have pigeonholed the novel in the same way.

22. C D Narsimaiyah, quoted in Mukherjee, 38.

Notes

CHAPTER 4

1. Edward Said, "Opponents, Audiences, Constituencies, and Communities," in W J T Mitchell, ed., *The Politics of Interpretation* (Chicago: University of Chicago Press, 1983), p. 28.

2. Margaret Laurence, "The Perfume Sea," in Malcolm Ross and John Stevens, ed., *In Search of Ourselves* (n.p.: J M Dent, 1967), pp.201-227.

3. Laurence, p. 221.

4. Laurence, p. 217.

5. Brent Harold, "Beyond Student-Centred Teaching: The Dialectical Materialist Form of a Literature Course," *College English* 34 (November 1972), 201.

6. Richard Ohmann, *English in America: A Radical View of the Profession* (New York: Oxford University Press, 1976), pp. 59-60.

7. Richard Abcarian and Marvin Klotz, eds., *Literature: The Human Experience* (New York: St Martin's Press, 1973), p. xiii.

8. Barbara Bailey Kessel, "Free, Classless and Urbane?" *College English* 31 (March 1970), 539.

9. Northrop Frye, *Anatomy of Criticism: Four Essays* (Princeton: Princeton University Press, 1957), pp. 347-348.

10. Terry Eagleton, "Ineluctable Options," in *The Politics of Interpretation*, p. 380.

CHAPTER 5

1. These concepts are presented in Annette Kuhn's *Women's Pictures: Feminism and Cinema* (London: Routledge & Kegan Paul, 1982).

2. Peter Abrahams, *The View from Coyaba* (London: Faber & Faber, 1985), p. 117.

3. David Lean interviewed by Harlan Kennedy, "I'm a Picture Chap," *Film Comment*, January-February, 1985.

4. E M Forster, *A Passage to India,* ed. Oliver Stallybrass (Harmondsworth: Penguin, [1924] 1986), p. 164.

5. *A Passage to India,* p. 164.

6. *A Passage to India,* p. 296.

7. *A Passage to India,* p. 39.

8. "I'm a Picture Chap," 32.

9. Michael Sragow, "David Lean's 'Rite of Passage'," *Film Comment*, January-February, 1985.

10. Letter to *The New York Times*, Toby Volkman, reprinted in *Southern Africa Report*, June 1985, 20.

11. Volkman, 20.

12. Ngugi wa Thiong'o, *Detained: A Writer's Prison Diary* (London: Heinemann, 1981), pp. 34-38.

13. Isak Dinesen, *Out of Africa* (Harmondsworth: Penguin, [1937;1954]1985), p. 64.

14. Reported in *India Abroad* by A Sikri, June 24, 1986.

15. *A Passage to India* pp. 314-315.

CHAPTER 6

1. Earle Birney, "Bear on the Delhi Road," *Ghost in the Wheels: Selected Poems*

(Toronto: McClelland & Stewart, 1972).

2. George Woodcock, "The Wanderer: Notes on Earle Birney," in *Perspectives on Earle Birney* (Downsview, Ont.: ECW Press, 1981), p. 97.

3. Although Birney does not use the terms "cruelty" or "brutal" in the poem itself, the following quotation suggests that that is how the scene impressed itself on him: "In the summer of 1958 I had a glimpse of a bear and two Kashmiri men on a roadside in northern India--seen from my passing car. It was a strange sight, of course, but it haunted me for reasons far beyond oddness. The bear was huge, shaggy, Himalayan. It must have been captured high up in the cool mountains and purchased by these men with perhaps the savings of their lifetime, and they had been walking with it hundreds of miles through mountain passes down to the terrible mid-summer hot plains, brutally training it for dancing as they went, so they could make a living exhibiting it in Delhi. But it wasn't just the bear's wretchedness, it was the two men's; it was their fearful, dumb hopping around the bear." "Madness and Exorcism of Poetry," in *Earle Birney,* ed. Bruce Nesbitt (Toronto: McGraw-Hill Ryerson, 1974), p. 196.

4. Birney, "Madness and Exorcism of Poetry," p. 196.

5. Samuel Taylor Coleridge, "Dejection: An Ode," *The Poems of Samuel Taylor Coleridge* (1912; rpt. London: Oxford University Press, 1964), p. 365.

6. Birney, "Preface," *Ghost in the Wheels: Selected Poems* (Toronto: McClelland & Stewart, 1977), p. 10.

7. Birney, *The Cow Jumped Over the Moon* (n.p.: Holt, Rinehart and Winston, 1972), p. 72.

CHAPTER 7

1. Kathy Mezei, "Speaking White: Literary Translation as a Vehicle of Assimilation in Quebec," *Canadian Literature* 117 (Summer 1988), 13. Mezei is here presenting the views of Chantal de Grandpre in "La canadianisation de litterature quebecoise: la cas Aquin," *Liberte* 159 (juin 1984), 50-59.

2. Mezei, 20-21.

3. See Chapter 3 of this book, "The Vocabulary of the 'Universal': The Cultural Imperialism of the Universalist Criteria of Western Literary Criticism."

4. "Introduction," *The Third Vow and Other Stories* by Phaniswar Nath Renu, trans. Kathryn Hansen (Delhi: Chanakya Publication, 1986), pp. 7-8.

5. "A Note on the Translations," *A Strange Attachment and Other Stories* by Bibhutibhushan Bandyopadhyay, trans. Phyllis Granoff (Oakville: Mosaic Press, 1984), p. 17.

6. Benedict R O'G Anderson, "Introduction,"*In the Mirror: Literature and Politics in Siam in the American Era,* ed. and trans. Benedict R O'G Anderson and Ruchira Mendoines (Bangkok: Editions Duang Kamol, 1985), p. 87.

7. D G Jones, "Text and Context: Some Reflections on Translation with Examples from Quebec Poetry," *Canadian Literature* 117 (Summer 1988), 6.

8. Renu, "Purani Kahani: Naya Path," *Aadim Ratri ki Mahak* (Delhi: Radhakrishna Publications, 1967), p. 71.

9. Renu, "Ucchatan," *Aadim Ratri ki Mahak,* p. 108.

CHAPTER 8

1. Margaret Atwood, "Introduction," *The New Oxford Book of Canadian Verse in English,* ed. Margaret Atwood (Toronto: Oxford University Press, 1982), p. xxxi.

2. Himani Bannerji, "Paki Go Home," *Doing Time* (Toronto: Sister Vision, 1986), p. 15.

3. Krisantha Sri Bhaggiyadatta, "Big Mac Attack!," *The Only Minority Is the Bourgeoisie* (Toronto: Black Moon, 1985), n.p.

4. Dionne Brand, *Primitive Offensive* (Toronto: Williams-Wallace, 1982), p. 32.

5. Joy Kogawa, *Obasan* (Markham: Penguin Books, 1983), p. 126.

6. Maria Campbell, *Half-Breed* (Toronto: McClelland & Stewart, 1973), p. 97.

7. Arun Mukherjee, *Towards an Aesthetic of Opposition: Essays on Literature, Criticism & Cultural Imperialism* (Stratford: Williams-Wallace, 1988).

8. Linda Hutcheon, "Complicity and Critique: The Canadian Postmodern," *Essays in Canadian Irony: Volume 1,* ed. Linda Hutcheon (North York, Ont.: Robarts Centre for Canadian Studies, York University, 1988), p. 64.

9. Marlene Nourbese Philip, "Oliver Twist," *Thorns* (Toronto: Williams-Wallace, 1980), p. 6.

10. Claire Harris, "Policeman Cleared in Jaywalking Case," *Fables from the Women's Quarters* (Toronto: Williams-Wallace, 1984), p. 38.

11. Frantz Fanon, *Black Skins, White Masks* (New York: Grove Press, 1967), p. 229.

CHAPTER 9

1. Robert Kroetsch, Tamara J Palmer, and Beverly J Rasporich, *Canadian Ethnic Studies* 14, no 1 (1982), iv.

2. The term *South Asian* is applied to denote immigrants who either have come to Canada directly from the Indian subcontinent (i.e. India, Pakistan, Bangla Desh, and Sri Lanka) or have ancestral links with the subcontinent. Thus, many Caribbean immigrants to Canada are descendants of indentured labourers from northern India who were lured there by the British in the nineteenth century.

3. Bharati Mukherji, "An Invisible Woman," *Saturday Night* (March 1981), 36-40.

4. Insofar as Michael Ondaatje's work does not speak of his otherness and visibility, he is excluded from this article. Elsewhere I have commented on these omissions in his work. See Chapter 11 of this book.

5. Cyril Dabydeen, "New Life," *This Planet Earth* (Ottawa: Borealis Press, 1979), p. 64.

6. *Canadian Ethnic Studies,* iii.

7. S Padmanab, "Night-Song," *Songs of the Slave* (Cornwall, Ont.: Vesta Publications, 1977), p. 26.

8. Asoka Weerasinghe, "Sahelia," *Poems for Jeannie* (Cornwall, Ont.: Vesta Publications, 1976), p. 27.

9. Arnold Itwaru, "Shattered Songs," *Nebula* (1st Quarter, 1981), 55.

10. Krisantha Sri Bhaggiyadatta, "My Family," *Domestic Bliss* (Toronto: Domestic Bliss, 1981), pp. 9-10.

11. Himani Bannerji, "Terror," *A Separate Sky* (Toronto: Domestic Bliss, 1982), p. 25.

12. Rienzi Crusz, "The Sun-Man's Poetic Five Ways," *The Toronto South Asian*

Review 1, 1 (1982), 54.

13. Lakshmi Gill, "Song," *First Clearing (an immigrant's tour of life) poems* (Manila, Philippines: Estaniel Press, 1972), p. 6.

14. *Canadian Ethnic Studies*, v.

15. Bhaggiyadatta, *Domestic Bliss*, p. 23.

16. Sukhwant Hundal, "A Letter to a Friend," translated from Punjabi by Surjeet Kalsey, *Toronto South Asian Review* 2, 1 (1983), 77-78.

17. Uma Parameswaran, untitled poem, *Toronto South Asian Review* 1, 3 (1982), 15.

18. Kenneth Burke, *Permanence and Change: An Anatomy of Change* (New York: Bobbs-Merril, 1935), p. 90.

19. Suniti Namjoshi, "Poem Against Poets," in Diane McGifford and Judith Kearns, ed., *Shakti's Words: An Anthology of South Asian Canadian Women's Poetry* (Toronto: TSAR Publications, 1990), p. 62.

20. Bannerji, "A Savage Aesthetic," translated from Bengali, *A Separate Sky*, pp. 46-47.

21. Dabydeen, "Lady Icarus," *Goatsong*, p. 16.

22. Suniti Namjoshi, "Philomel," *Feminist Fables* (London: Sheba Feminist Publishers, 1981), p. 102.

23. Itwaru, *Nebula* 1st Quarter (1981), 54.

24. Salman Rushdie, *Shame* (Calcutta, Rupa, 1983), pp. 38-39.

25. Raja Rao, "Foreword," *Kanthapura* 2nd ed. (Madras: Oxford University Press, 1974), p. v.

26. Dabydeen, "For the Sun Man," *Elephants Make Good Stepladders* (London, Ont.: Third Eye, 1982), p. 51.

27. Surjeet Kalsey, "Siddhartha Does Penance Again," *Toronto South Asian Review* 2, 1 (1983), 75-76.

28. Parameswaran, "Ganga Jal," typescript received by this author from the poet. Subsequently published as "Chandrika" in McGifford and Kearns, ed., *Shakti's Words*, pp. 75-77.

29. Ioan Davies, "Senses of Place," *Canadian Forum* (April 1982), 34.

CHAPTER 10

1. Sam Solecki, "Michael Ondaatje," *Descant* 14, 4 (1983), 78.

2. *Ibid.*, 79.

3. *Ibid.*, 78.

4. Michael Ondaatje, *The Man with Seven Toes* (Toronto: Coach House Press, 1969).

5. Ondaatje, *Coming Through Slaughter* (Toronto: Anansi, 1976).

6. Ann Wilson, "*Coming Through Slaughter*: Storyville Twice Told," *Descant* 14, 4 (1983), 103.

7. *Ibid.*, 103.

8. Quoted in Donald M Marquis, *In Search of Buddy Bolden: First Man of Jazz* (Baton Rouge and London: Louisiana State University Press, 1978), pp. 109-110.

9. Ondaatje, *The Collected Works of Billy the Kid: Left Handed Poems* (Toronto: Anansi, 1970).

10. Ondaatje, *Running in the Family* (Toronto: McClelland & Stewart, 1982).

11. Qadri Ismail, untitled review, *Kaduwa* Journal of the University of Ceylon, 1 (1983), 44-45.

12. Yasmine Gooneratne, "Cultural Interaction in Modern Sri Lankan Poetry Written in English," in G Amirtanayagam and S C Harrex, ed., *Only Connect: Literary Perspectives East and West* (Australia: Flinders University, 1981), p. 186.

13. *Ibid.*, p. 189.

14. Rienzi Crusz, "Faces of the Sun-Man," *Elephant and Ice* (Erin, Ont.: Porcupine's Quill, 1980), pp. 35-36.

15. Crusz, *Singing Against the Wind* (Erin, Ont.: Porcupine's Quill, 1985), p. 70.

16. *Ibid.*, p. 60.

17. Crusz, *Elephant and Ice*, p. 94.

18. *Ibid.*, p. 90.

19. Asoka Weerasinghe, *Home Again Lanka* (Ottawa: Commoner's, 1981), p. 26.

20. Weerasinghe, *Poems for Jeannie* (Cornwall, Ont.: Vesta Publications, 1976), pp. 58-59.

21. Krisantha Sri Bhaggiyadatta, *Domestic Bliss* (Toronto: Domestic Bliss, 1981).

22. Bhaggiyadatta, *The Only Minority Is the Bourgeoisie* (Toronto: Black Moon, 1985), np.

23. Charles Altieri, *Enlarging the Temple: New Directions in American Poetry During the 1960s* (Lewisburg, Pa.: Bucknell University Press, 1979).

24. "October 25, 1983: Invasion of Grenada," *The Only Minority Is the Bourgeoisie.*

25. Tyrrell Mendis, *Broken Petals* (London: The Mitre Press, 1963).

26. Ranjini Obeyesekere and Chitra Fernando, ed., *An Anthology of Modern Writing from Sri Lanka* (Tucson, Ariz.: The University of Arizona Press, 1981).

CHAPTER 11

1. Ondaatje, *The Dainty Monster*, 1967; *the man with seven toes*, 1969; *The Collected Works of Billy the Kid: Left-Handed Poems*, 1970; *Rat Jelly*, 1973; *Coming Through Slaughter*, 1976; *There's a Trick with a Knife I Am Learning to Do: Poems 1963 to 1978*, 1979; *Running in the Family*, 1982.

2. Dabydeen, *Distances*, 1977; *Goatsong*, 1977; *Heart's Frame*, 1979; *This Planet Earth*, 1979; *Still Close to the Island*, 1980; *Elephants Make Good Stepladders*, 1982.

3. Douglas Barbour, "Controlling the Jungle," *Canadian Literature* 36 (Spring 1968), 86.

4. Whitney Balliett, *The New Yorker*, Dec. 27, 1982, 76.

5. Michael Ondaatje, *Rat Jelly* (Toronto: Coach House, 1973), p. 62; hereafter, the collection is referred to as *RJ*.

6. Ondaatje, "Walking to Bellrock," *Capilano Review* 7 (Spring 1975), 126.

7. Charles Altieri, *Enlarging the Temple: New Directions in American Poetry During the 1960s* (Lewisburg, Pa.: Bucknell University Press, 1979), pp. 18, 20.

8. Sam Solecki, "Nets and Chaos: The Poetry of Michael Ondaatje," in Jack David, ed., *Brave New Words* (n.p.: Black Moss Press, 1979), p. 24.

9. Frank Lentricchia, *After the New Criticism* (Chicago: The University of Chicago Press, 1980), pp. 53, 55.

10. Solecki, "Nets and Chaos," p. 47.

11. Lentricchia, p. 54.

12. Robert Lowell, "Imagination and Reality," a review of *Transport to Summer*, *Nation*, April 5, 1947; rpt. in *Wallace Stevens*, Penguin Critical Anthologies (Harmondsworth: Penguin, 1972), p. 155.

13. Meredith Tax, "Introductory: Culture Is Not Neutral, Whom Does It Serve?" in Lee Baxandall, ed., *Radical Perspective in the Arts* (Harmondsworth: Penguin, 1972), p. 16.

14. Lentricchia, pp. 57-58.

15. Roland Barthes, *Mythologies*, trans. Annette Lavers (New York: Hill and Wang, 1972), pp. 100-102.

16. Sam Solecki, "Point Blank: Narrative in Michael Ondaatje's 'the man with seven toes'," *Canadian Poetry* 6 (Spring/Summer, 1980), 14.

17. Solecki, "Nets and Chaos," p. 29.

18. Colin MacInnes in Kenneth Clark, et. al., *Sidney Nolan* (n.p.: Thames and Hudson, 1961), p. 22.

19. Ondaatje, "O'Hagan's Rough Edged Chronicle," *Canadian Literature* 61 (Summer 1974), 24.

20. Raymond Williams, *The Country and the City* (1973; rpt. Frogmore, Herts.: Paladin, 1974), p. 24.

21. Williams, *The Country and the City*, p. 214.

22. Ondaatje, *Running in the Family* (Toronto: McClelland & Stewart, 1982), pp. 85-86.

23. Quoted by Thomas R Whitaker, "Poet of Anglo-Ireland," in John Hollander, ed., *Modern Poetry: Essays in Criticism* (New York: Oxford University Press, 1968), p. 413.

24. Cyril Dabydeen, *Goatsong* (Ottawa: Mosaic, 1977), p. 28; hereafter referred to as *G.*

25. Michael Hurley, *Canadian Literature* 89 (Summer 1981), 167.

26. Ron Miles, *Canadian Literature* 87 (Summer 1979), 138.

27. Quoted by Eric Homberger, *The Art of the Real: Poetry in England and America Since 1939* (London: Dent, 1977), p. 142.

28. Dabydeen, *Distances* (n.p.: Fiddlehead, 1977), p. 10; hereafter referred to as *D.*

29. Dabydeen, *This Planet Earth* (Ottawa: Borealis, 1979), pp. 41-42; hereafter referred to as *TPE.*

30. Dabydeen, *Elephants Make Good Stepladders* (London, Ont.: Third Eye, 1982), p. 48.

31. Quoted by Altieri, *Enlarging the Temple*, p. 63.

32. Quoted by M Adereth, *Commitment in Modern French Literature: Politics and Society in Peguy, Aragon and Sartre* (New York: Schocken Books, 1968), p. 19.

33. Dabydeen, letter to author.

34. Ondaatje, "Moving to the Clear," an interview with Jon Pearce in *Twelve Voices: Interviews with Canadian Poets* (Ottawa: Borealis, 1980), p. 135.

35. Arnold Rampersad, "The Universal and the Particular in Afro-American Poetry," *CLA Journal* 25 (September 1981), 8.

CHAPTER 12

1. Rienzi Crusz, *Flesh and Thorn* (Stratford, Ont.: Pasdeloup Press, 1974).

2. Crusz, *Elephant and Ice* (Erin, Ont.: Porcupine's Quill, 1980); hereafter cited in this essay as *EAI.*

3. Crusz, *Singing Against the Wind* (Erin, Ont.: Porcupine's Quill, 1985); hereafter cited as *SAW.*

4. Margaret Atwood, "Introduction," in Margaret Atwood, ed., *The New Oxford Book of Canadian Verse in English* (Toronto: Oxford University Press, 1982), p. xxxi.

5. "Editorial: On Visibility," *Canadian Literature* 95 (Winter 1982), 2-5.

6. Robert Kroetsch, Tamara J Palmer and Beverly J Rasporich, "Editorial: Ethnicity and Canadian Literature," *Canadian Ethnic Studies* 14, no 1 (1982), iii.

7. Myrna Kostash quoted in Jars Balan, ed., *Identifications: Ethnicity and the Writer in Canada* (Edmonton: The Canadian Institute of Ukrainian Studies, The University of Alberta, 1982), p. 151.

8. Crusz, "Sitting Alone in the Happy Hour Cafe," *Still Close to the Raven* (Toronto: TSAR, 1989), p. 13.

CHAPTER 13.

1. Rohinton Mistry, *Such a Long Journey* (Toronto: McClelland and Stewart, 1991), pp. 10-11.

2. John Clement Ball, *Paragraph* 13, 3, 29.

3. Ball, 29.

4. Clark Blaise, *The Globe and Mail*, May 4, 1991.

5. Philip Marchand, *The Toronto Star*, May 4, 1991.

6. Ball, 29.

7. For example, Marchand, *The Toronto Star*.

8. Val Ross, *The Globe and Mail*, November 30, 1991.

CHAPTER 14.

1. Neil Bissoondath, *Digging Up the Mountains: Selected Stories* (Toronto: Macmillan of Canada, 1985).

2. V S Naipaul, *The Middle Passage* (1962; rpt. Harmondsworth: Penguin, 1969), p. 28.

CHAPTER 15.

1. Ven Begamudré, *A Planet of Eccentrics* (Lantzville, BC: Oolichan, 1990).

CHAPTER 16.

1. M G Vassanji, *Uhuru Street* (Toronto: McClelland and Stewart, 1992).

CHAPTER 17.

1. M G Vassanji, "Introduction," *A Meeting of Streams: South Asian Canadian Literature* (Toronto: TSAR, 1985), p. 2.

2. *Ibid.*, p. 3.

3. Frank Davey, *Post-national Arguments: The Politics of the Anglophone-Canadian Novel Since 1967* (Toronto: The University of Toronto Press, 1993), p. 97.

4. Arun Mukherjee, "The Exclusions of Postcolonial Theory and Mulk Raj Anand's *Untouchable*: A Case Study," *Ariel* 22, 3 (July 1991), 27-48.

5. M G Vassanji, *The Gunny Sack* (Oxford: Heinemann, 1989), pp. 10,14.

6. Robert G Gregory, *India and East Africa: A History of Race Relations within the British Empire 1890-1939* (Oxford: Clarendon Press, 1971), p. 5.

7. Gregory, p. 1.

8. Quoted in Gregory, p. 91.

9. Vassanji, *No New Land* (Toronto: McClelland and Stewart, 1991), pp. 22-23.

10. C A Bayly, *Indian Society and the Making of the British Empire* The New Cambridge History of India II, 1 (London: Cambridge University Press, 1988), p. 5.

Acknowledgements

The articles and essays published in this book have appeared previously as credited below:

"The Vocabulary of the 'Universal': The Cultural Imperialism of the Universalist Criteria of Western Literary Criticism," *World Literature Written in English* 26, 2 (1986), 345-52.

"Ideology in the Classroom: A Case Study in the Teaching of English Literature in Canadian Universities," *Dalhousie Review* 66, 1&2 (1986), 27-39.

"The Third World in the Dominant Western Cinema: Response of a Third World Viewer," *Toronto South Asian Review* 5, 3 (1987), 3-11.

"On Reading Renu: /Text/Language/Culture/Translation," *Toronto South Asian Review* 8, 1 (1989), 59-69.

"Ironies of Colour in the Great White North: The Discursive Strategies of Some Hyphenated Canadians," Linda Hutcheon, ed., *Double-Talking: Essays on Verbal and Visual Ironies in Contemporary Canadian Art & Literature* (Toronto: ECW Press, 1992), pp. 158-171.

"South Asian Poetry in Canada: In Search of a Place," M G Vassanji, ed., *A Meeting of Streams: South Asian Canadian Literature* (Toronto: TSAR, 1985), 7-25.

"The Sri Lankan Poets in Canada: An Alternative View," *Toronto South Asian Review* 3, 2 (1984).

"The Poetry of Michael Ondaatje and Cyril Dabydeen: Two Responses to Otherness," *Journal of Commonwealth Literature* 20, 1 (1985).

"The Poetry of Rienzi Crusz: Songs of an Immigrant," *Currents* 4, 1 (1986-87).

"Narrating India, Rohinton Mistry's *Such a Long Journey*," *Toronto South Asian Review* 10, 2 (1992).

"*A Planet of Eccentrics*: Ven Begamudre's Fantastic India," *Toronto South Asian Review* 10, 2 (1992).

"M G Vassanji's *Uhuru Street*," *Paragraph* 14, 3 (1992).

THE AUTHOR

Arun Prabha Mukherjee came to Canada from India in 1971 as a Commonwealth Scholar at the University of Toronto. An Associate Professor of English at York University in Toronto, she is the author of *The Gospel of Wealth in the American Novel: The Rhetoric of Dreiser and His Contemporaries* (1987), *Towards an Aesthetic of Opposition: Essays on Literature, Criticism and Cultural Imperialism* (1988), and numerous articles on postcolonial literatures, women's writing and critical theory. She has edited an anthology of writings by women of colour and aboriginal women entitled, *Sharing Our Experience* (1993), and contributed entries on several South Asian women writers to *A Feminist Companion to Literature in English* (1990).